The Gushungo Way
poems

The Gushungo Way
poems

By

Ndaba Sibanda

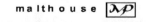

Malthouse Press Limited

Lagos, Benin, Ibadan, Jos, Port-Harcourt, Zaria

© Ndaba Sibanda 2019
First Published 2019
ISBN: 978-978-56219-7-6

Published and manufactured in Nigeria by

Malthouse Press Limited
43 Onitana Street, Off Stadium Hotel Road,
Off Western Avenue, Lagos Mainland
E-mail: malthouselagos@gmail.com
malthouse_press@yahoo.com
Tel: +234 802 600 3203

Distributors:
African Books Collective Ltd
Email: abc@africanbookscollective.com
Website: http://www.africanbookscollective.com

Dedication

In memory and honour of those who were persecuted or those who perished in pursuit of justice and *who they are*.

Acknowledgements

The author thankfully acknowledges the publications and places where the following poems have previously appeared:

"A Clumsy Flimsy Flip-flop" in Scarlet Leaf Review, January 2017

"A Dinner Prayer" in Page & Pine, April 2018

"A Doctor Of Dictatorship" in Football of Fools blog, March 2018

"A Soul In Solitude" in Piker Press, September 2014

"As If They Didn't Know" in Scarlet Leaf Review, January 2018

"At It Again" in Poetry Potion, March 2013

"At Long Last" in Piker Press, January 2017

"Bhalagwe" in Poetry Potion, November 2017

"Bring Back Our History and Heritage" in Scarlet Leaf Review, October 2016

"Finally" in Piker Press, January 2018

"From City To Rusticity" in Whispers, February 2014

"Haunted By His Mentor`s Disastrous Ghost" in Piker Press, December 2017

"It Is Theirs, Please Do Not Ruin It Any" in ITCH, February 2017

"Nyaope-Ruled" in Scarlet Leaf Review, April 2015

"Not Even A ..." in Scarlet Leaf Review, April 2018

"Of Policies And Capacities" in Piker Press, April 2016

"Of Sycophantic Peacemakers" in Piker Press, February 2018

"Placards" in No Achilles, July 2015

"Rising To The Challenges Of Today" in Scarlet Leaf Review, February 2017

"Rising To The Challenges Of Today" in Winning Writers, November 2017

"Roar Into Life" in NonDoc January 2018,

"Roar Into Life" in Scarlet Leaf Review, January 2018

"Shenanigans" in Football of Fools Blog, April 2018

"Sleeping Rivers" in Page & Pine, April 2018

"The Drunk`s Sober Words" in Piker Press, April 2016

"The Lake Of Vice And Valour" in Piker Press, July 2015

"The Ramshackle Bus" in Poetry Potion, September 2014

"The Time Is Here" in Randomhouse , March 2018

"The Time Is Here" in Scarlet Review, April 2018

"There Is A Method To Her Madness" in Unlikely Stories Mark V, July 2016

"Walk A Mile In Their Shoes" in The Criterion, February 2017

"Wondering about Nocturnal Wanderings" in Scarlet Leaf Review, January 2018

"Wonders Will Never Cease" in Universidad Complutense de Madrid, July 2016

"Willowy Words" in Scarlet Leaf Review, April 2017

"Unswayed Folly" in Scarlet Leaf Review, February 2017

"Unswayed Folly" in Winning Writers, November 20017

THE POEMS

Roar Into Life

it`s better to give us a plate
full of fried bitterness than
too much sugar because
that causes fat droplets!

it was as if I were listening
to a team of tough-talking
health and fitness experts
but those were editors!

they ranted: speak rawness
into the truth about life
stretch our capacity
for compassion

test our understanding
enter the heart of what
we cherish or cheapen
and interrogate it madly

I knew then that the narrative
was never going to be a sleep-
inducing affair anymore
but a wake-up call

I Don't See Them Here

I wish I could see them here in Zim
In the north and south in Zim, they don't zoom
In Luanda where I lived their ubiquitousness
Smiled in the north and south or west and east

I wish I could see them here in Zim
In the north and south in Zim direction is dim
Hence cranes are like the thighs of a tortoise
No one sees sheaves being lifted or stirred!

In other countries I have visited or lived in
Overhead cranes were in action and everywhere
In Zim those industrial machines are not ubiquitous
Like many other things their *development* is disingenuous!

In the supermarkets they used to have items which were labelled
Made in Zimbabwe: those were our produce, our pride, our exports
But not anymore, they vanished: *where's your choice beef?* they ask
I wish I could give them a more reasonable answer than *sanctions*!

Acidic Assimilation Sermons

They preached plastic integration
With an astonishing passion

As if they expected their roguish dreams
And the victims` noble ideas to kiss osmosis

Of Sycophantic Peacemakers

They dump their dummies in Mthwakazi
Ceremonial and titled string-puppets

They are playing with the poor victims`
Minds and emotions on a muddy turf

It`s the perpetrators` hideous game
Of pretending, pushing and duping

Those they thrust into the chess chest
Are too sheepish and dollish to move

Because they are remoted to act
As if they are placid frogs and birds

That inflate their throats with lies
And chirp fooling songs of healing

And a very virgin reconciliation
A clear promotion of gimmickry!

It Cannot Be Defied

idiocy comes in many forms
as lifeless jokes and snake holes
lapdogs are good at flouting rules
in their bid to ingratiate and gratify
but on this ageless fact people say be civilized
enough to accept that no person born of a woman
can rewrite the rules of nature no matter how cruel!

Bhalagwe

urns of bigoted carnages
gaze into their nude decadences

justice refuses to wink or decay
truth cannot be crushed or cremated

Crying Out For A Holistic Change

He spoke as if his utterances
Were a harbinger of bounty

A kind of pragmatic prophecy
A river well for the thirsty

He trampled on the past
And its poverty and drought

But people wanted his words
Impregnated into clouds of now

They had eaten a lot of past promises
And were hungry for a real transformation

Actions Awaken People

On polished platforms
They preach perfect peace
But sadly they practise perfidy

On paper there is progress
On the ground they digress
They peddle lies and wars

What they stir up
With their elECTIONS
Are some defECTIONS

Lost Cultural Compass

Their traditional song
Was loud and long

It was about the roles
Of chiefs and a king

In a modern- day society
Wreaked by decadence

The song was about the restoration
Of a people`s dignity and identity

The song was about the restoration
Of Mthwakazi`s lost history and heritage

A Precise Presence

A superstar with a big skill of expressive speech
Catch her confidence and fluency and accuracy
An accent heaving with honey and clarity
What a particular way of speaking
Action-packed delivery and diction
Intonation and elocution
No further explication
Thokozile!

Necessary Tools In A Fast-paced World

I heard and saw critical and creative thinkers
Trying to put their chain of curiosities to work
A trio of language and content and thinking
There was a series of open-ended questions
Did 15 billion dollars just vanish into thin air?
Did the locals from Manicaland benefit at all?
Where were the eyes and ears of government?
Will the culprits be hauled into parliament or jail?
A prediction here and a description there
A reflection here and an extension there
I heard the assured voices of educators
I heard the philosophers and politicians--
All were crazily consorting with the art
And science of astute thinking
Mine was an observation

A Better Future Or A Blasted Bet

Her tears taunted her mind
As they cascaded down her face
She had staked on the new suitors--

A crew that had crept in via the back door
With pomp and a string of pretty promises
Her wager on them was fast fading into blues

Her team of Nicodemuses was loaded and unhallowed
Their wealth of experience in the affairs of life and love
Didn't charm her a bit her but then she sought after a Canaan

Inflated Dread

His dreadlocks a perturbation
In the presence of some office snobs

Each time the quiet attorney entered the office
There was a high measure of hyperbolic uneasiness

Stereotyped whispers of 'Bhinya' were loud antics
As if he were a mighty mythical scruffy bush terror

Corporate Cruelty

The world`s biggest listeria outbreak
Exposed the unscrupulousness and heartlessness
Of some big and powerful companies in South Africa

Poor people perished after eating mainly cold food
Which was suspected to be contaminated
Losses that could have been avoided

A Slim Slingshot Boy

It sounded fictional. But it was not
folkloric. The boy had a slingshot.

It looked harmless under his bed--
but not when he used it. It nibbled.

When his parents were away
he became a proverbial weasel.

They say the weasel is at ease
when the mamba has gone away.

What a possession. What an obsession.
He griped the projectile in the pouch.

The boy`s bowhunting skills came
to the fore as he took an aim…

Then he raised his slingshot and pulled
the band back. A poor passer-by screamed!

Children In The Cold

There is no delight
when one catches the sight
of them. There is a nerve's flight.

Chances of a better future
are not rosy. Fewer and fewer.
Young, there is no loser cuter.

Chances of a little education
are slim. Stared by starvation.
Stabbed by uncultured socialisation.

Their little toys are breathing obscenities
as they dance on street fights and activities.
They pester people's peace and sensitivities.

Woman of Today

Enjoying the amenities and peculiarities
of modern living
of dynamism

Clamouring for greater marital power
at household level
at national level

Denouncing a subordinating social position
in any given locale at any given time
in any given space at any point

Basking in the prospect of reigning supreme
over patriarchal fanaticism
over male pig chauvinism

Engrossed in a conversation to give credit
to women's reproductive and productive powers
to women`s empowerment rightists and entities

Vowing
never to accept oppression as if her hands were tied to her back
never to accept tokenism in business and in politics and in education

A woman of today says no
to the trammels of culture and religion
to an inferiority complex or pull-her- down syndrome

A woman of today
seeks to be treated as an equal at a workplace
seeks to read the epitaph of oppression and degradation

Elusive Pumpkins

Dear dear Sun
Please please send your princely rays
Down down to heat Sea and Dam
Lovely lovely live-in parents of Water

So that Water delivers Son Vapour
Who might therefore ascend to Sky
To condense and come down refined--
Talk of a lively dance of Rain and Grain

....

The clouds are gathering in the sky
A darkness looks near but is high

I hear children singing *Woz`Malamlela*
Come down Rescuer
Singing *Woz`sidle amakhomane*
Come and let`s feast on pumpkins

For the young children understand well
That when Nature has smiled on the land
People grow lush fields with pumpkins
And everyone jives into jollity and plenty

Rain do not refrain
Please enough of pain
Come down today
Come down Rescuer

Fields are rumbling with emptiness
Sadness defaces farmers` faces

As they see no vegetation
But a fist of sickening starvation

Industry long came to a heavy halt
Life is starved of economic salt

Rain do not refrain
Please enough of pain

Come and let`s feast on pumpkins

Two Sides of the Horizon

on one hand quitters cry
a castrated chant

they capitulate
and emasculate their spirit

on the other champs charm
mere reveries into rare realities

down the road deserters demotivate
up or down the road victors advocate

Cool And Calm In The Midst Of Storms

From where Sikhona stood it seemed as if her father
Obediently acceded to all her step mother`s requests

From expensive jaunts within and without the borders
Of the country to dresses and food, she had her way

From where Sikhona stood it seemed as if her father
Openly endorsed her enslavement and persecution

Sometimes he would walk in and find the whip shelling
Her skin and her tattered dress -but turn a blind eye on it

How many times was she humiliated and chased out
Of school owing to unpaid school fees? Did she cry?

Did he ever ask why she was too slim, decent and reticent?
Sikhona had taught a stoical acceptance of her sorrows

In fact her sorrows whose tomorrows haunted her soul—
Served to confirm her victimhood to an imposed orphanage

Semester

she had to forego pleasantries
and get down to serious business

she had to be steady and studious
for it was a time to get ahead of the game

Just A Friendly and Frank Chat

As far as Mandla was concerned
His mom was cracking a chestnut

The boy did not find all this amusing
The mother thought she was advising--

When he came back from college he knew
She would utter pleasantries and platitudes

"I`m tired of my mother`s starting and parting remarks"
Mandla decided to confide in his best college friend

"What exactly is the matter with her statements, my friend?"
Asked Mandla`s pal behind the wheel of a fairly good Honda Fit

"The moral content of her remarks smacks of something that has
been used too often to be motivating or thoughtful or relevant"

Mandla responded while his friend listened as he steered the car
"She cares for you, she bought you this car, and this is how you thank her?"

What Doesn't End Is Surely Ominous

From the outset many people in and around Bulawayo
Disapproved of his party and his ascendancy to the throne

It was as if they could feel that his Johnny- come- lately elevation
To the highest office in the land was bound to be a nightmare

Bulawayo, Matabeleland Provinces and parts of the Midlands
Wore mournful faces after the announcement of poll results

No sooner had the first black president of the country
Consolidated his power than he started to make cruel forays

Power has a way of sizzling like an eternal fire of glory
Aristocracy fizzles out like morning dew on blades of grass

Supremacy is a thin fooling sphere of liquid enclosing shitty air
Sometimes the has-beens fail to come to terms with reality

During his heydays he called himself a revolutionary icon
He looked into his mirror: boom an invincible superman!

A manipulator of the constitution, a, suppressor of opposition
A seizer of power and prestige, a master of violence and fear

"Countries don`t get bankrupt! "he jeered when asked if by
Rushing troops to Congo in 1998 would not hurt the economy

Prime land and other benefits belonged to him, to his wife,
His generals, his acolytes, his cabinet ministers, his cronies

If you were a journalist and you criticized him as being unfit
To rule, then you became a sell-out, and an enemy of the state

Poor souls were arrested for no bigger a "crime" than to describe
Him as an "old man", for he defined himself as young old man!

The trappings of power saw him pronounce woes to souls
Who dared to advise him or to criticise his iron-handed ways

And anguish he unleashed without hesitation or restraint
Using the organs of government which were at his disposal

By the same token, if one were a Ndebele and one complained
Of unfair treatment, one became a recipient of gratuitous LABELS

Through a history and a culture of mistrust, hegemony and bigotry
One was labelled a tribalist or a dissident or a foreign –among others

Of course that stereotyping drive was aimed at the isolation, silencing,
Degradation, submission, frustration and assimilation of the victims

The Gukurawundi crimes against humanity left him with the gloomiest stain
On his track record and a scar that plagues the country up to this very day

His brutal and far-reaching domestic spy network was a human rights
Blow, and a legacy of economic and social ruin as citizens fled the nation

If one were a woman leader from Matabeleland and one raised eyebrows
About what one deemed an unfair incident-- objectification snowballed!

All Hell loose, one was not only reminded that one was a dissident or foe
One became an object of sex – a Ndebele harlot-- as witnessed recently

All that politicisation of everything, all that tribalisation of the political
Space is his legacy as it was his subtle pastime with his comrades in arms

If the West dared to criticize him for human rights violations
He was quick and decisive: *you`re a racist, to hell with you!*

If a Ndebele criticized him for a situation in which a local
University had 95% per cent of the lecturing staff from outside

The region, and those teachers because they sought to assert
Their superiority, and knew they were no repercussions

They tended to use their mother tongue gratuitously -Shona instead
Of English to conduct lessons, on hand, say, the same institution

Had imported 98% of students from Mashonaland - condemning
The local youth to ignorance: the criticizer became a barred tribalist!

The criticizer was condemned, criminalized and called a divionist
Yet the government was pursuing and practising divionist policies

Some of his party members or his tribesmen luxuriated in their
Over-glorified superiority and illusions even on national radio!

People complained of a scenario where almost all the schools
Colleges and business entities were owned or run by people

From outside the province - or where teachers who could
Not string a few words into a sentence in the local language

Were, year in year out recruited from outside to teach
Students, let alone grade one learners—but all was futile

If one criticized him then one had applied to be labelled
And dismissed as a traitor or a sell-out or a puppet or a foe

If one were a Ndebele and one formed and led a political party
No matter how inclusive or big it could be, it was REGIONAL!

Such parties and their leaders were demonized and delegitimized
He ridiculed them as divisive elements, or snakes or local minions

When the president was a darling of the former coloniser,
The former leader of ZAPU was listed as his worst enemy

Years later when another opposition leader gained political mileage
The president teased him as a teaboy, not stating *he* himself

Used to be a teaboy of the West, who dined with the big guns big time
Observers say he managed to get away with Gukurahundi murders

Partly because he was bedfellows with the West before the farm captures
He was known to be a proud perfectionist for ceremony and detail

Add that to an unadulterated Western style of dress and his use of English
And to his penchant for travelling to the West, especially his regular visits

To upmarket department stores in London: then you get an Anglophile who
  liked

A gravy minus its constituents "I would be a rotten thinker to think like
  them."

Hair-dyed, his heart and mind seemed to be there in a big way
As he frequented the home of Britain's best bespoke tailors

And guess, what –he might not have been a British clone
Or thought like them, but had a Western feel to his dress code

During the graduation ceremonies in Zimbabwe he wore academic
Regalia used in some of Britain's most old-fashioned institutions

Not only did he have a British conservatism about his appearance
He confessed to adoring a British sport of cricket like no other

Of it he enthused "it's a game every young Zimbabwean should
Learn to play. It is a civilising influence". What else? Well…

  The one who struck real and perceived foes with fear and disgust
Because his brutality and egotism brooked no opposition or person

As far as he was concerned the country had to be liveable
And lovable in spite of hunger and brutality he visited on it

The one and only who was Head of State and Government
And commander in chief of the defence forces, yet those

Who opposed him became lackeys of the West or saboteurs
Their crime was of lamenting the magnitudes of his misrule
  The most powerful, the most revered, the first and the last
The one and only conferrer of hero status in the entire nation

The one and only who, through his reign and leadership style
It dawned on citizens that *succession* was not a mere word

His response to a reporter about the possibility of grooming
A successor was" I did not say I was a candidate to retire."

The one who reminded people that succession was not "our"
Culture and likened grooming a successor to an inheritance

The citizens realised a new dimension to the use of that term
It turned out to be a punishable sin to utter that word in public!

The aspirants to the throne knew the sacredness of that word
They were smeared or kicked out in spite of their elusiveness

The one who had the sole right to send cold-blooded vultures
To crush and silence real or imagined enemies without a trace

The one whose rallies were to be attended and bowed down to
By school children, even if most of whom were apolitical or aloof

Yes, the one who prioritised the preponderance and maintenance
Of roadblocks rather than the upkeep of the nation`s road networks

Yes, the one who was thought to be the nation itself and the party
At the same time, and treated both like his private property

One who, possibly, thought of himself as more of a feudal king
Than a modern president in a world of modernists and reformists

If ever he saw himself as a president, then through his manoeuvres
It can be reasonably assumed that he wanted to be a life president

Some analysts contend that he had every reason to cling on in
Spite of his infirmities and fiascos by virtue of fear of justice

Asked who would succeed him, at 92 he queried "Why successor?
I am still there. Why do you want a successor?" Not him!

He drove his point strongly by asking the interviewer: "Do you
Want me to punch you to the floor to realise I am still there?"

One who faced general opposition to his authoritarian rule
Resulting in a 2000 constitution referendum defeat for his party

February 2000 saw his government taste a surprise loss as its
Constitutional review proposals were rejected by the citizens

Then the war veterans went on a rampage as they engaged
In violent farm invasions under the hyped honeyed banner of

The so-called 'fast track land resettlement programme'
That happened on the backdrop of his administration `s

Failure to craft and adopt an all-encompassing veterans'
Policy for the former fighters` re-integration back into society

A lack of a fair, meaningful and maintainable programme
To assist the veterans as part of their disarmament,

Demobilisation and re-integration into society was always
Bound to engender political uncertainty, instability and chaos
The farm occupations were characterised by violence, anarchy
And lawlessness directed at white farmers and their property

In all the drama surrounding the post-independence land invasions
There was a titanic supremacist fallacy that was widely publicised

By the government and some partisan media houses on who actually
Had started "the revolution" for land and in which part of the country

Just like the first war of uprising against white settlement and rule
Members of the radical Inqama Settler`s Association were the pioneers

Well before the world heard about the land invasions in Mashonalamd
The Inqama settlers occupied government farms in the Matobo area

It was in Matobo in Matebeleland that the landless people rampaged
For land, and had running battles with the police before 1997

They resisted an eviction order, and were arrested but vowed to return
The Inqama leaders were an unsung group of fearless activists

The Inqama`s sole sin in a politically polarised country was that
Theye were not regionally, ethnically and politically correct—simple!

So much for a president who presented himself to the rest of the world
As a no-nonsense pan-Africanist champion and a unifier of Africa!

 He presided over a system that propped up triumphalist and supremacist
Egoists and beneficiaries, yet expecting complacency from the victims!

Years later when farm occupations started in Mashonaland
His government did not show any highhandedness and resistance!

By the same token the same government did not only denigrate
And undermine the role played by the ZIPRA forces in the liberation war

The fact that First Matabele War was fought between 1893 and 1894
Seemed to have been deliberately downplayed by pro-ZANU historians

Known as the Battle of the Shangani,, it pitted the British South Africa
Company, which had about 750 troops, and an unknown number of colonial

Volunteers assisted by about 700 Tswana allies--against King Lobengula`s
80 000 spearmen and 20 000 riflemen, armed with Martini-Henry rifles

 British South Africa Company's Police and their allies were victors
 To mark their victory, they nailed the company flag and the Union Jack to a
tree

It is instructive to see how same the government treated the two scenarios

For the same reason the first war against colonialism was falsely portrayed

In history books as if the first liberation war began in Mashonaland!
Learners were fed with appalling untruths and mythical exaggerations

 One who vetoed his conscience to own his mountain of privileges
And the entitlement of one group at the expense of other citizens

One who, in spite of widespread poverty threw lavish parties
And awarded huge pay rises to the MPs and cabinet members

The one who used government apparatuses and personnel
With extreme brutality and fear to keep himself in power

The one who knew how to unleash violence and propaganda
To preserve his grip on power in spite of targeted sanctions

The one during whose reign it was apparently not a taboo
To grease govt workers` palms in order to get things done

The one to whom it was ostensibly a crime or an insult
To challenge in the ballot box or to criticise constructively

The one who *knew* how to Hitlerize the public broadcasting
Station and government-owned papers into echoing his voice

The one who had the right to parcel out all land and justice
The one who had the right to withdraw all those privileges

The one who independently chased away white saboteurs
The one and only guardian of people`s freedom and land

If his moral bearings were lost during the Gukurahundi atrocities
Then his economic plot plunged into oblivion with farm seizures

The political capitulation of ZAPU and its support base could
Have made him an ethnic cleansing maestro, but not a business star

The massive unbudgeted payouts dished out to the war veterans
Also created a financial scramble which had economic repercussions

As powerful politicians, senior government officials and other players

In the country`s liberation war became applicants and happy recipients
Owing to loopholes and corrupt tendencies the sad part about the gratuities
Was the alleged draining of the national fiscus of millions of dollars

Through inflated compensation claims for disabilities which the applicants
Claimed they had sustained during the period of the armed struggle

The one who some much surrounded himself with bootlickers
That he was spoilt for choice when it came to *job-blessing*!

Though bootlicking was no automatic license to promotion
The long-suffering citizens felt bootlickers were unsympathetic

To their plight and blind to the sad realities on the ground
To his lapdogs, the Machiavellian politician was everything

Some observers contended that the president thrived on praise-singing
That bootlicking paid off for those who had amazing bootlicking skills

Whether he reduced adults to pathetic turncoats or some people
Just had a penchant for bootlicking? -- are questions citizens asked

A church leader once compared him to Moses and a prophet whilst
A Masvingo Provincial Affairs Minister described him as a king

Some citizens, especially the Christian community, were angered,
They believed the president`s idolizers had sank to irredeemable levels

A former city manager equated him to Jesus and for all his fawning
Antics, guess what, he was rewarded with a deputy ministerial position!

"Our Angel Gabriel", quipped a toadyish former youth secretary at
The president`s rally for the youth attended by jobless, cashless souls

"Gushungo, people say you have Cremora, the whole body. The war the
World over is about you. They fear you, that`s why they`re doing all this"

That was a Provincial Affairs minister upping his gear of hero-worshiping
Without doubt, he was of the president`s biggest praise- singers and defenders

People heard what they thought was idolatry and sycophancy gone askew
He added that the president's grandson too was "Cremora"-- a milk brand!

 An apple-polishing party political commissar said as a liberator
The president should rule for a long time and, yes, as long as he saw fit!

Generally viewed as an antithesis to tourism and democracy, his former
Tourism Minister strangely called him a centre of tourism development!

This was in spite of the fact that the tourism industry was in distress
The president`s absurd demagogic outbursts did not help the situation

A Higher Education Minister described him as one of Africa's all-time
Greatest men envied for his "encyclopaedic" memory, wisdom and courage

Not to be outdone perhaps was his party`s secretary for administration—
Before things turned sour, and so nasty that they threw live snakes at each
other!

Before their dramatic fallout, the loyal secretary had described the president
Not only as a messiah but also as the best thing that has happened to Africa!

"A messiah sent by the Almighty to lead Africa in general and Zimbabwe
 In particular to gain their land back", deified the ex-State Security minister

The bandwagon of praise- singers included some musicians too
In fact some of them carved out their careers through glorifying him

The president was nicknamed Robbery after the 2008 elections
Electoral defeat was too bitter and shameful a taboo for him

 Regarded as a shameless vote-rigger and a plotter of one
Of the greatest electoral thefts in history he romped into a fake win!

After demonstrating that he meant serious business by upping
His game of violence and butchering prior to the run-off election!!

Of course to protect the so-called gains of OUR independence
And the sovereignty of the country, elections had to be RIGHT

When he declared, "We'll win, we`ll be winning all the time", he meant it!
He did not mince words, "Only God who appointed me will remove me"

Political scientists blamed it on his inflated political ego and the fear
Of prosecution for graft and a mountain of crimes against human

The intelligence agents were notorious for their cruelty and ubiquity
Turned into despicable human rights violators, they were abhorred

When some foreign leaders expressed their unhappiness over
His tyranny, he was quick to remind them of territorial integrity!

Never mind the common thread which characterized the polls:
Misuse and monopoly of state media, abuse of traditional leaders

For the opposition, the game was lost before the kick-off whistle
In the various prisons and villages as his 'big' party bulldozed all

The opposition doubted the neutrality of the Electoral Commission
And the registrar general's office`s management of the voters roll

In the early years of power-sharing, the opposition spent energies
Fighting for appointments to ministries, not pushing for reforms!

There was a president who knew that elections had to be RIGHT
Their lack of credibility, fairness and transparency was no big issue

 Forget the noises about his legitimacy or international diplomacy
What was clear was that elections had to be won at all costs

That life and limp were lost seemed not to bother him a hoot
Let alone if such victims were not his card-carrying followers

That the hand of law was selective and cynical was loud and clear
Villagers could not attend freely pre-election meetings of their choice

To push bloc voting down the hands of vulnerable poor villagers
The military, the police, the militia and the war vets to bullied voters

It was payback time for the new black farmers as threats of eviction
Were directed at resettled families if ever they voted the WRONG way!

He scoffed at critics who called such elections as nothing but a scam
When there was an election or his star rally people had to be active!

The bussing in of people from other constituencies was a notorious tactic
Observers bemoaned what they saw as high numbers of assisted voters

Voters roll was said to be doctored, voter registration purposely skewed
His party officials were no strangers to dabbling as electoral umpires
Sometimes they were caught with a bunch of counterfeit registration slips
At times the PATRIOTS dabbled in keeping fake ink and in double voting!

Despised for ruining one of Africa's most promising economies,
He blamed it on sanctions on state firms and travel restrictions

His party rocked by factionalism, he was known to be a man
Who resorted to divide and rule tactics to affirm his leadership

His wife stood by him, saying the centre of power was one
Together they outfoxed, together they waxed and waned,

Instead of being regretful about the de-industrialisation
And pauperisation of Bulawayo, he resorted to attacks

He attacked the people from Matabeleland for the great trek
To South Africa in search of menial jobs and little blankets
On the other hand she took "Ndebele bulls by the muscular tail"---
Saying they were not interested in progress but in polygamy!

"It is common here to find a man with 5, 6 or 10 wives,
What kind of a bull is that?" she asked and derided in Gwanda

The generality of the Ndebele men and women were piqued ---
They were of the opinion she was the least qualified to say that

She had nicknames associated with luxury and violence,
She was dubbed 'Gucci Grace' and 'First Shopper'

Those two monikers were in honour of her lavish lifestyle,
She spent lavishly on garments, mansions, cars and jewellery.

Also labelled Marujata, meaning a *troublesome woman*
She disgracefully flogged a model in a South African hotel suite!

'Doctor Stop It' was briefly detained by police in Singapore
After she assaulted reporters, tossed their mobile phones into a pond!

Seeking to dishearten those who were angling to take over from her
Frail and failing husband, she told the attendees he was irreplaceable

And that he would rule even after he was interred at the Heroes Acre –
She claimed as a God-chosen president, he would rule from the grave!

Said, a praise-worshipping former vice president singing for his supper,
"You`re as good as the president, so you must be addressed as Her
Excellency"

Coming from one of the minorities, he was not only regarded as a big dummy
But also as a traitor, yet he was content being number three in the presidium!

Against a tradition that forbids a man from kneeling before a woman,
A cabinet minister made himself a joke when he bowed down before Grace!

Her political soap opera rose on the back of political kowtowing and
hypocrisy
Said her aide 'She`s angel sent by God to help long-suffering Zimbabweans"

Those were the self-styled saviours and philanthropists
Who plundered as much as they purported to aid

Those were the greedy charlatans and rabble-rousers
Who preached development and did dirty destruction

Those were the self-styled unifiers and peace-makers
Who orated on unity and peace but thrived on tribalism

As the loud claimants of PanAfricanism they butchered,
Ridiculed and persecuted fellow Africans with impunity

They balked at tackling their awful human rights violations
They were unwilling to acknowledge the presence of skeletons

As unrepentant masters of arrogance and prejudice
They dismissed Gukurahundi atrocities as madness
Yet incontrovertible historical and political evidence
Puts the man as one of the main architects of that lunacy

It is a known fact that the Chihambakwe Commission which was set up
To pore over the Gukurahundi saga, did its work and compiled a report

Similarly the Dumbutshena Commission came out with its report,
Yet curiously, those two crucial reports have been swept under the rug!

The findings of those two Commissions have remained a mystery
Just like the disappearances of some human rights activists

The verdicts of those two Commissions have remained a mystery
Just like the torturous abductions of some opposition party members

To the Gukurahundists their supremacy was no bubble
Innocent villagers were sacrificed on the altar of dissidence

If indeed it was an issue of dissidents, why did the soldiers
In some instances, force the victims to pronounce Shona words?

And those who failed such a 'test' were selected and killed!
Did people`s inability to speak Shona make them dissidents?

How were horrific mass-murders of the innocent, unarmed civilians
Going to aid in the defeat or elimination of the dissidents?

If the government wanted to wipe out the so-called dissidents
Why was the killing of innocent and unarmed the order of the day?

They failed to explain why they formed a North Korean-trained unit
To commit a genocide in which more than 40 000 Ndebeles died

They ran and sustained sinister, subtle and well-coordinated activities
Aimed at assimilating, annihilating other people culturally or physically

They shamelessly abused educational and broadcasting institutions
They institutionalized corruption, propaganda raped professionalism

Other citizens` rights were systemically violated: their languages,
Histories and the history of the liberation war –were all butchered

They frowned upon other people`s cultures and existence
No wonder they undermined other citizens` sense of worth

People from other tribes were treated as second class citizens
They could only become vice presidents, a perpetuated disparity

He created a system of tokenism where a few bootlicking puppets
From the minority groups were given senior cabinet and party positions

Those little bootlicking beneficiaries, became the locals` worst traitors
As they became his bellowing toy bulls, his overzealous spokespersons

In line with an African in idiom," Don`t talk when eating" those appointees
Knew where their best interests lay and defended their master`s bigoted
    practices

One provincial minister, like a number of leaders from Matabeleland in his
    party
Even loudly absolved the president of his well-documented crimes against
    humanity

He castigated individuals, political parties and civic organisations which were
calling

Upon the president to address the issue of perennial underdevelopment in
Matabeleland

He claimed it was a myth peddled and promoted by Western diplomats and
foreign-funded
Political parties, taking advantage of the big gap after the passing away of
ZAPU`s leader

He also absolved the president of the chaotic and costly land grabs, claiming
he had respected
The provisions of the Lancaster House Constitutional Agreements which
specified that

The land redistribution was to be carried out on a willing seller- willing buyer
basis
During the first ten years of independence, so the president`s hands were tied
to the back!

What he did not touch on was why the president had not acted after the ten-
year moratorium
He buttressed the widely-accepted view, that the president was the West`s
trusted teaboy

Until the advent of the farm grabs---by saying not only did his dear president
receive
Standing ovations from Western Europe and the USA, they also pampered
him with

Several doctorates with the hope of pulling him away from pursuing his noble
Liberation struggle goals, namely of achieving political and economic
freedom!

All that untenable clowning was aimed at securing himself a seat on the gravy
train
One former defence minister from Matabeleland and a fanatic founding
member

Of ZANU allegedly invited an eternal rejection and ire from the Ndebeles
After declaring that he wished he had a way of washing off his Ndebeleness!

That was how low some Ndebeles had to stoop in order to be trusted and
accepted
Into the president's hegemonic and historically tribalistic party—a whole loss
of self!

The other cynical political game he probably perfected and played was the
creation
And financial nourishment of a bunch of sham political heavyweights and
whores!

The president and his grand planners followed their sectarian policies to the
book
They created a working class from their majority, and beggars from the
minorities

In the 1990s it was not easy to question the status quo because the
government
And the majority of beneficiaries shot down any hint of discontent or
discrimination

For the minorities, be it in government or private, in education or business the
best
Level they could attain was being deputy this or vice that—what an abnormal
norm!

A mere greeting in one of the minorities` languages could stir up arrogance
and
Superiority as one from the ruling class usually responded "Handinzwisise"

Good morning sir or madam, *I don`t understand,* "What don`t you
understand?"
"Handinzwisise" *(I don't understand)"* was a national disaster, a cossetted
malady

Discerning human rightists blamed the malignant *Handinzwisise Malaise* on
supremacists
It was a result of their aversion and reluctance to promote citizens and
languages equally

It was an open secret that language controversies and inconsistencies rocked
the nation
Wrong language in parliament, passports, adverts, on TV and radio –a futile
storm!

For the majority had no business knowing, let alone speaking the minorities`
lingoes
But if the minorities said the same about the majority, a crime was
committed!

He also created a subtle situation where the members of the majority group literally
Invaded the spaces and villages of the minorities in an arbitrary and greedy way

When the unfavoured complained over the plundering of their local resources,
Or the closing down or relocation of companies—he couldn't care less

For hegemonic and tribalistic reasons, Gwelo became Gweru,
Selukwe was changed to Shurugwe, so was Mbelengwa etc

Intoxicated with ethnic supremacy they implemented
Their evil 1979 Grand Plan clandestinely and extensively

One day in Bulawayo disgruntled residents defaced signs and traded
A street named after him with one indicative of their grave concerns

Troubled about perennial underdevelopment and discrimination
They covertly changed Robert Mugabe Way to Devolution Way!

Up to this very day most of the Bulawayans want that street
Name changed as its presence is a nagging nail in their flesh

Not only because he regarded them as an uneducated group of
Malcontents and irritants who deserved to play second fiddle

They also associated its existence and essence with nothing else
But an unholy celebration of the butchering of their relatives

The two enjoyed a first status which by an error of destiny
Could crown them the first vicious incorrigible bigots and felons

The country sank and sank into paucity and distress
As corruption and mismanagement became endemic

But they believed they had innate finesse and grace
They thought that they were born to rule forever

Their appetite for power and self-righteousness
Saw them craft a self-grown *demoncracy*

Their hunger for dehumanizing and demonizing
Voices of dissent was felt and seen on the scene

What kind of parents were they --when they clearly had their favourite
Daughters and sons whom they promoted and protected at all costs?

Those daughters and sons were the uncontested beneficiaries of companies,
Mines, education, employment and business opportunities across the country

That scenario created a serious social, cultural, political and economic time
    bomb
Most of the beneficiaries, for their part in the rot, never raised a dissenting
    voice

  They became gainfully employed, educated, socially and politically
    influential
---If not superior –and in most instances worked tirelessly to maintain the
    status quo

While his divide- and- rule tactics made him a hero in sections he was
    pampering
Protecting with tenders, executive jobs, companies and company relocations,
    etc.
 They became truly and finally untenable when the economy took several
    nose-dives
By virtue of mismanagement ---plunging the beneficiaries into dire straits as
    well

Even the best of blueprints aimed at the promotion of sustainable economic
    growth
And poverty alleviation become an exercise in if there is no political will but

Too much political expediency, if there is little or no implementation but
    rhetoric
Grandstanding, if the principles of management are ignored to cover up
    corruption

That was the case-- the president had an impenetrable proclivity for shielding
Those who were found on the wrong side of the law, sometimes he
    completely

Overrode or ignored findings of the anti-corruption commission
Or literally rescued the favoured culprits from prosecution or arrest

Economists impressed on him to desist from putting politics ahead economics
On issues of policy implementation but all those pleas fell on deaf ears

The president`s myopic arrogance translated into a huge economic liability
Instead of reengaging the world he relied on one side under the Look East
 Policy

As the political landscape deteriorated, some musicians whose praise-singing
 songs
Used to rule across national airwaves and other gigs, also fell from fortune to
 famine

Some artists who had benefited from aligning themselves with his party
 realized
That the pastures were no longer green, and went overseas and slammed him
 sweetly!

As citizens sank into an abyss of social anguish, a lot migrated to SA, UK, US
 and other
Nations, and a once 'hit song' *The Blair That I Know Is a Toilet* was flashed
 down too!

Of that song, one youth bawled, "I'm suffering because myopic bundlers who
 can`t even
Man a mere Blair toilet were entrusted with the managing of the nation.
 Stinking nonsense!"

One legendary singer whose revolutionary songs extolled the virtues of the
 ruling party
And the president but vilified Nkomo`s ZAPU-- seemed to have had a change
 of heart

Unlike other artists who masked their political lyrics, he became one
Of the ruling party's biggest critics and the president`s fallen admirer

Some of his songs were banned on radio because those were no longer
Telling "defeated Nkomo to shut up", but bemoaning disasters and rags!
Unjust harshness which used to be meted out on the ridiculed sufferers
Was gradually extended to the favourites as they grumbled about decline

Alien to the rule of law, democracy, democratic processes and institutions,
A semblance of the independence of the judiciary was a bitter pill for him

Equally, the holding of internationally –observed elections was a tall order
In 2002 the nation was expelled from the Commonwealth for election
 violence

Their spin doctors kissed the ground
They walked on, including all the filth

They frantically colonised all spheres of govt,
Organs of govt operated as their private entities

As the first born members of aristocracy
They did not want anything with a shabby air

Hence Operation Murambatsvina was a campaign
 To forcibly clear slum areas across the country

 Was it not degrading to have dirty street kids
In the presence and glare of international dignitaries?

That is why they bussed off dirty street vagrants
Before any international conference in the city

At the climax of their self-worshipping delusion
Was a passion for pontificating and purging

In the conquest of her beauty the woman sang
Songs of her elegance, and other`s nonsense

A stop –it, stop- nonsense discourteous firebrand
Full of herself, everything revolved on her whims

She had several flights, fights, farms under her belt
A self-appointed heroine, a selfless worshiper of self

She politicized everything she could lay her eyes on
She persecuted perceived foes and factions

She was intoxicated with power and pleasure
While her man thought everyone was his puppy
War vets once described him as a genocidal dictator
Who thought he had a prerogative to insult other people

One who boasted of having degrees in violence, insulting
Opponents was a pastime: hell, cows, dogs, braying mules

His peccadilloes and persecution of opponents marked
His presidency, his rabble-rousing was unpresidential

Conscienceless linear thinkers and bootlickers even said
He had an age-ability to go against the rules of nature!

Short of scooping the coveted *Corruption Prize For Ruining*
Short cuts, shady dealings and kickbacks embodied their admin

They left behind crumbs and decay, gifts of impoverisation
 The mineral rich country was viciously raped and run down

In the process the poor found themselves having to queue
For everything: food, money, bearer cheques, bond notes

He denied that the country was in the throes of bankruptcy
And an economic meltdown even when the writing was there!

In July 2008 it had the world's fastest-shrinking economy and
An annual inflation of 231 million per cent—a clear catastrophe!

To their credit they made citizens poor owners of millions,
Trillions and zillions—an unprecedented hyper-inflation

Any party or person who criticized their party`s actions and policies
Was quickly termed a puppet of the West or an enemy of the people

A South African veteran anti-apartheid campaigner, and a Nobel Peace
Prize Winner joined mounting international criticism over his leadership

"He seems to have gone bonkers in a big way. It is very dangerous when you
Subvert the rule of law in your country," observed the famous clergyman

He said the sensible thing for the country`s leader was be to step down
That was after his party, enjoying a comfortable majority, had passed

Two controversial laws: one that criminalized criticism of him
And surrendered sweeping security powers to the government

And another that banned independent election monitors
And denied voting rights to millions of the citizens living abroad.

South Africa, notorious for its policy of quiet diplomacy broke its
Silence said it was "unacceptable" for the country`s army to signal

That it would only accept a victory by him in the presidential polls
The Nobel Peace Laureate advised Mbeki`s government to adopt

A stronger stance as his quiet diplomacy had failed, and he knew that
Our president was facing a serious election challenge from the MDC

The churchman added, "When you don't even respect the judgments
Of your judges...then you are on the slippery slope of perdition"

Faced with growing international isolation, the government had
Vowed to accept international observers, but strictly on its own terms

In November 2017 when he sacked his vice president and right hand man
In a dramatic, deceptive effort to hand power to his wife, things backfired

There was widespread speculation in the country and beyond that his
    presidency
Was being prepared as some feudal monarch for none other his vocal wife

The military stepped in and put him under house arrest, and his grip
On power experienced a litmus test for the first time in 37 years

 November 15 saw the military take a bold and surprise move,
Crowds and crowds took to the streets in support of the army officers

The officers stepped in under the aegis of targeting criminals around him
Clearly he felt let down by SADC or AU or South Africa and "allies"

The world`s oldest leader was not going to give up power easily
The nation was stung by a cloud of political uncertainty in the belly

On 21 November 2017 after defying demands to step down
For close to a week after a military takeover and expulsion

From his own ruling party the tyrant made a decision to resign
As parliament heard a motion to impeach him, a cornered man

His departure was received with wild cheers at a special session
Of parliament as the speaker read out his resignation letter
His ouster sparked scenes of euphoria in the capital city as the
Crowds cheered, danced and sang in praise of the military

He later stated, "I was pressured by the army to resign"
The military seized power under "Operation Legacy"

After his removal several members of a group allied to his wife
Were arrested and expelled from the ruling party by his long-time ally

What the nation needed was a new era, a break from brutality,
From repression of dissent, from election rigging and vote-buying

What the citizens desired was democracy and constitutionalism
They were tired of being victims to a man-made economic flop

They were fed up with the ruling party but then the new president
---Nicknamed "the crocodile" from his liberation war time--- was

A senior ruling party official who was associated with the former
Head of state's unmatched brutality and destruction for the last 37 years

Many people did not consider him as someone with a pair of clean hands
He definitely was not an admin in a WhatsApp group of democrats either

He was a member of the former strongman's inner circle since liberation
He was the ex- leader's security chief during the Matabeleland massacres

The army officers were the same people who a few years back had vowed
Never to salute an opposition president without any liberation war credentials

Described as his miniature, his enforcer and faithful lieutenant and confidant
After assuming power, perhaps his success was the removal of roadblocks

Seeking to run away from the shadow of his master and mentor, he called
His government a new dispensation but skeptics termed it a new deception

Whilst the pre-election period was comparatively peaceful, if the opposition
Leader made things eerie or tricky by declaring himself a presidential winner

The army turned the situation into a tragic outrage when they had unleashed
    live
Ammunition on unarmed, rowdy demonstrators in the capital city

A place where a few months ago citizens had hailed the soldiers as liberators
1 August 2018 did not only see the capital city resemble a war zone, a pariah
    state

But also it saw the blatant disrespect for the sanctity of life by the authorities
6 people lost their lives, reminding the world of the horrors of the ex-
    strongman

Indeed the ex-strongman had a reality show on which the actors
Were none other than Starvation, Desolation and Depression

The poor were constantly told to be patient, patriotic and loyal
Tighten your belts they preached whilst floating in luxury and pomp

For medical treatment and entertainment, foreign nations babied them
While the poor patients were condemned to public hospitals without drugs

The poor state of the public health institutions and road networks
Was a mark of their misplaced priorities and their insensitiveness

Yet they thought the people and the country owed them—
They thought they owned the people and the country

If ever there were heartless demons or devils in the world
Most people in Mthwakazi would point fingers at them!

The kind of decay and damage the two left behind doesn't
Need a rocket scientist to see, acknowledge or quantify

Instead of prosperity and peace they left behind a country
Torn apart by mistrust, polarisation, pretence and poverty

My Two Ideal Worlds

If ever there was an ideal world
It would be within earshot --
Without a gunshot

I suppose it would have—
Acres and acres of pages
Lyrics and love and letters

Wedded to melodies
Seasoning life
Even in strife

Music my intimacy
A depth of emotions
Even in commotions

Without it
The world is lonely
Even hellish & hollow

Without it
My heart is hungry
Even uneasy

For it is easy
On my ears
As it seizes my fears

Through it
I touch love
An aroma of life

Therefore
Sing me a song
So real and ideal

Wedded to writing
Words my loyalty ring
Text my certificate and king

To write is right
For it`s a weapon
For justice and literacy

Not Even A …

Did you see the medical doctors stage a demonstration?
Hear there was a solution without any documentation!

Didn't they say politicians should use government hospitals?
Hear government is failing to procure drugs and essentials!

Didn't their placards read something like "monster of health"?
Hell, something about perennial failures and politicians' wealth!

Didn't they say the old *new look* nation is open for business?
However closed for health! This is horrible. And I'm SERIOUS!

Didn't the *tired* doctors denounce a certain CEO who has a jeep?
Hell, I guess because poor patients don`t have a single drip!

Strolling Eyes

eyes…
explore this enchanting island
like a romantic tour

On The Wall

Could he have had something bewildering?
Something like a nightmare. Foreboding.

Could he have had something a bit suspicious?
Something like smiling snakes. Speaking spears.

Maybe, just maybe he didn't think about it.
That the pool could have been deep. Fiddly.

Maybe, just maybe, the pool was calm. Plain.
Its waters clean. You could drink them up fine.

Gwenya knew he could bite snakes. As always.
He knew too that he was incapable of drowning.

Gwenya buried his head under a rug. As always.
Yet it was imminent. An unwelcome change.

Gwenya had a deficiency. No decency but denials.
Gwenya drowned in them. Dehydrated, drank vexation.

He drank dryness like a lost fish. No dyeing. It was like dying.
Where was the omen? The phenomenon that foretells the future.

Caught In Between

In this context, in this discourse,
 we are not talking of a contraction
 of *between* or something like that.

We are discussing the wearing
of inaptly short skirts and shorts
by our youngsters, our tweens.

We discussing how to handle those
 between 10 and 12 years of age
who are howling with friends---

As if, on one hand, are angry to be
considered too old to be children---
on the other, too young to be teenagers!

The Debate Rages On

ever thought of chiefs
and village heads?

of presidents
and chief executive officers?

one activist said these positions
don't come on a silver platter

women –be hungry grabbing lions
journalists-- write about one`s character

why do you tend to dwell on non-essentials?
like she is a divorcee or a single mom with two kids

ever thought of nurses and caterers or care-givers
without seeing a misleading picture of women only?

A Doctor of Dictatorship

big and bizarre human rights scandals
committed by some African regimes

normalcy is showing the weaknesses
or diseases of old age or wild tantrums

about a lack of democracy when you know that
in all your life you have been alien or allergic to it

victims of gukurahundi massacres clamour for justice
they bay for his blood like the victims of Gambia's former leader

insisting on justice after being used as guineafowls-- as he forced people
with HIV to undergo treatment with a herbal concoction he had invented
    himself

A Dinner Prayer

His father went on and on
About blessings and food
For almost six minutes

Both parents had their eyes
Closed and their mind focused
But not their boy, their only child--

He thought of the dinner appeal
As too long, and himself as too weak
To deal with salivating lips, an empty belly

When his parents finally whispered their 'amens'
And opened their eyes, Bongani`s plate was already
Half-empty, his cheeks dancing, vibrating with chewing

Tough Choices

A transitional period full of issues. Controversies.
Challenges of independence and self-identity.

Biological changes of puberty. Dramatic.
Cognitive changes come with concepts.

Adolescents and their peers and parents.
Teens and parents sometimes conflict.

Over many issues--schoolwork, drugs.
Socialisation, sexuality, alcohol, love.

If the right choices are not made: woe
Could come in as depression or suicide.

Shenanigans

There is so much hype about it
Much noise about a nil or a naught

The hysteria on listeria is sincere
It is worth all the efforts and attention

Not the naming and shaming tricks played on us
It is a spoofed movie on getting raiders exposed

The film is titled: Externalisation Versus Imitation
It is a hoax that will not snap on the heels of saboteurs

What a piece of parody and paradox good people!
Let he who hath not sinned cast the first stone

Cultural Centre

It was a weekend of inspiration and revival
The Centre took away my nagging nakedness
And clothed me with the charms of tradition

The charms of tradition echoed in their spaces
They exuded an African grandeur second to none
I felt the deepest desire to be myself and my mirror

What A Kind Of Kindness

Mr. Mlambo, a gifted Science Teacher
taught in the Kunene and Omusati regions
in Northern Namibia for more than ten years.

When he came back to Bulawayo I asked him
how his stint was in the Kunene and Omusati regions.
He talked about the beauty of the country in general,

and the hospitality of men to male visitors in particular.
He paused and smiled before saying he had lost count
of the occasions he was treated to *Okujepisa Omukazendu*.

"What is that treatment? "I inquired. He said it is a practice where
one`s wife is given to one`s guest to spend the night while the husband
sleeps in another room or outside. Floored, all I could utter was," Really?"

The Time Is Here

Riding on. Riding a tight rope.
Not healthy. A brutal history.

Suppression of dissent. Untenable.
The writing. It`s on angered faces.

It`s no longer cast in stone. Hell!
With blocked eyes, he rides on.

He sits on the pained backs
Of small birds tightroping.

Tightroping the lean line of life.
His self-centeredness sucks. Sick!

Can't you see the bloodshed?
Check the time. Pack. Kabila!!

How Can?

how can fairness thrive and live in pools that seek to
submerge it under their junk of anomalies and realities?

how can justice be just when the ghost of traumatisation
keeps on hunting the helpless victims and their families?

how can the world be human when human rights
and the sanctity of life are disregarded or disrespected?

how can there be unity when machinations of discrimination
and complicity are still used and funded with impunity?

how can there be transparency and democracy
and credibility when inconsistencies are the order of the day?
.

Dream

I dream of a better village
that will not fall victim
to abject poverty again,
because leaders could
not care less.

I dream of a better city
that will overcome the ills
of unemployment and corruption,
A lovely city whose resources will not
be looted and vandalised by predators
while the hapless residents feel like outsiders--
Because of little politics of prejudice and malice.
Please let there be lights again in that royal city.

I dream of a country whose name will no longer be
The Ruins-
A country whose citizens will be treated with dignity,
care and love.
I dream of a land where national positions and wealth
will not be issues of personal patrimony.
I dream of an Africa whose key responsibilities
will be to concretely put the people's aspirations
and choices above other considerations.
I have a great love for Africa, a hunger for its development,
a prayer for the proper utilization of its resources
and a thirst for justice and meaningful freedom.
I dream of a better continent and a peaceful world;
I dream of strong institutions, not personalities.

Servant Leader

Mr. Ndlangamandla was appointed
Minister of Indigenisation and Development.
The reshuffle saw many useless cabinet ministers
Being recycled as usual. Honourable
Ndlangamandla was a mafikizolo.
A new kid on the block.

It was the norm for them to
Make glorious promises about
Parachuting the poor out of their woes—
Parting company with the truth on a daily basis,
Losing themselves and their heads and humanity,
Claiming to have the ability to dig the desperate
Citizens out of their miserable financial graves,
And breathing into their lives pure sweetness—
Only to get into office and yawn all day long!

The other ministers--the reused lot--told him
Frankly that they had joined the party to get
Positions and loot like everyone else.
One minister said, "Our paradise is here. Those who fought
in the liberation war wanted us to live in the lap of wealth.
Anti-Corruption noises are to be ignored. Be blind
to whistle-blowers` noises. As long as we are loyal
to our seniors, we are immune like them.
We are rewarded no matter what evil we commit.
What more can one ask for?"

One of them added, "Rule number one,
shower our seniors with blind praises. Remember,
they are incapable of making errors! Rule number two,
don`t share party secrets with the opposition or the West.
 Rule number three, feast. You are Minister of what?
Development, right? Develop what?
Your family and a circle of friends and relatives.
 That's what it means. That's how we operate here.
 From the top to the bottom. We`re a looters` club.
This is free education. This is free information. Kickbacks
are our ball game we play very well. Grease palms for tenders.

There is nothing for nothing. Forget about the poor. Why lose sleep
over them? Are they your relatives? Didn`t you find them poor?
Yes, you did. So just feast. Feast in privacy, in public.
Yes talk about development."

Mr. Ndlangamandla could not believe what
he was hearing. He had been a technocrat overseas.
This was his opportunity to develop his country.
When others were falling over themselves
for the glamour and glitz associated with
their cozy jobs, he told the government to
sell the luxury car and uplift the poor…
He was walking the talk he had with the
taxpayers before the elections.

The recycled ministers then hated him
with a passion. Who did he think he was?
They queried among themselves,
planning his downfall.

Waiting

The people of Gwanda and Nkayi and Plumtree
innocently thought they held the key to success
until the charlatans told them that the lock
was nowhere to be found but in chicanery!

They were advised to wait (not in vain!) for
the road to success was under construction.
However, what they could see was destruction!

Soulless Souls

Is this a leaderless world

               where pariah antics are

a specialty?

No moral standards to talk about?

             No regard for lives

except for the worshipping of money and madness?
Where hooligans make a mockery of people and peace?

Hymn Book

Mnmm that opposition man…

Maybe he is on a pay roll…

Many people take with a pinch
of salt his politics of patronage.
His tongue is sticking out excitedly
for he is licking lumps of fatty rumps.
The people`s enemies are seduced
by his sugar-coated words and actions.
The opposition members ask,
Does he need a verbal diaper
for his vocal diarrhea?
He seems to be singing
from the same hymn book
with the notorious bullies.
Could he be supping
with the evil ones?

Driver's Licence

The maddening steering
wheel that stirs clouds
of controversy over the
horizon of hope and history.
With it,
they sweep, swing and swerve.
With it,
they lie, loaf and lull.

Driving to a graveyard
of rights and rules--
a standstill
of dissent, development
and democracy. Running
roughshod over voices
of progress and peace.

With it,
they slot, slay and slander.
With it,
they dine, dive and dodge--
leaving behind casualties
of horror, hunger and hate.

With it,
they love, live and lose.
With it,
they fool, flirt and flaunt--
up and down on their
yawning potholes
of fear, folly and fury.

At It Again

He travels with the largest delegation
ever to leave these shores.
Globe-trotting is his passion,
yet itching are the taxpayers' sores!

The Innocent Are Guilty

The ruling took every
Matobo resident by surprise.
A clear miscarriage of justice
against those under the siege of
the unknown settlers and invaders.

The Matobo villagers are bemoaning
the sinister seizure of their grazing land.
Dangerous daggers have been drawn…
Where will their children`s children
have land to graze or till or do rituals?

Moved to tears,
fights back tears,
as fears and fears
grow that those spears
will ripple off acquitted ears.

Be Wary of Snaky Ways

How can a snake be asleep?
When it wants you to weep?
Listen clearly to its venom sing.
Now it is time for logic to ring.

The Immunities of the Perpetrators

There is a bitter taste stinging the tongue with distaste.
The ghosts of atrocities haunt high and low for the masters of indignities.
The poor victims` cries fall on deaf ears.

The victims find themselves in an unrepentant pool of bruised memories.
The heartless slaughterers are feasting in couldn`t-care-less immunities
and in the lap of wealth.

Proclivities for rewarding evil are all over the corridors.
The passport instructions in the mother-tongue are littered
with deliberate grammatical and typographical impurities.

The land has known neither peace nor development. It is
littered with innocent grieving bones in shallow graves.
The villagers of Tsholotsho live in fear of genocide.

Citrus Farm

fruit is fun for sure
but what ensued
was fraudulent

when we were
young passing by
in a bus or a car

what we used
to marvel at
was your sight

what a spectacle
of lined greenness
singing production

the aroma of oranges
was stout and loud
in rich ESigodini

now there is the scary
odour of dying trees
crying redundancy

many a villager says
it is a sign of sabotage
others see betrayal

it stares us in the face
with sickening spikes
of shamelessness

dear citrus farm
please promise
you will not die

citrus fruit what
happened was silly--
suicidal tendencies
citrus fruit we all
long for your scent--

your great greenness

your juiciness we all
adored and extolled
as we exported you

can mouldiness shape up?
or it should just ship out
for freshness to jet in?

citrus farm come back
with your greenness
to restore our richness

The Drunk`s Sober Words

Those men and women are too drunk
to care about you and your plight.
Do you still believe they'll save you?
If you do then this is no longer a plight.
Like no action, it's none but your blight.
Can't you see they drive fancy cars?
At times brazenly on potholed roads!
Their destruction is far from being over.
When will you wake up from delusions?
If they wanted or could: you'd be better.
Honestly we`re stuck in their mess:
No currency, no cash, no jobs, no progress
Yet we have lots of companies that lie idle.
The ordinary man`s high ideals are rarely
Shared by these hopeless imps in power.
Why? Self-indulgence and self-interest rule.
They wine, dine, drivel, stagger or fly out
whenever it suits them and their coterie.
They say your problems come from far. Far?
Did people from far destroy your factories?
Tell me frankly, did they destroy commercial farms?
Don`t misquote me or get me wrong on this issue—
I didn`t say it was right and human for prime land to be
The privilege for a select group, whilst the majority
Of the landless indigenous folk sang sorrowful songs
in infertile villages or in crowded and crime-ridden suburbs.
I condemn that land anomaly as a huge travesty of justice.
That doesn't absolve these destroyers of their crimes. No!
 Are they not the ones who're heading govt agencies?
The non-performing agencies and getting hefty salaries?
Practicing nepotism and tribalism instead of good ethics?
Whenever there`s a funeral the company closes temporarily
Because the manager is related to every employee there!
Your problems: no jobs, no power, no growth.
Do they've the slightest idea of fixing these?
The rascals lie and tell you they're fixing them.
Or will it take them 202 years to fix them?
They use big geysers and electric heaters

and whirring fans but you don`t have
electricity and jobs and enough money
to keep your sober heads above water.
You call me drunk, yes, you're right!!
But I'm much better, I'm not drunk
with clout and corruption and frills.
Pan- Africanists, they claim? Yes.
How can you even believe that?
Such evil denial is genocide itself.
The black dead must be sobbing.

What The Economists Said

Low industrial production
              and liquidity challenges
              dog the country's economy
Mining sector woes
              entail costs of production
              costs of labour
              unreliable and limited
electricity supply
and high electricity traffics

Beneficiation and value addiction drive
              faces challenges
              of lack of skills
              and technology
The country's competitiveness is on the wane
              so said the economists

Of Policies and Capacities

this economy has whiskey
how can it be so drunk and risky?

the poor say the prognosis is easy
for this country has a terrible leprosy

termites and maggots of corruption
and governance constitute its destruction

police please arrest someone willy-nilly
for intoxicating this economy silly

policies please be competitive
for the businesspeople are restive

there is need for industrial production
as much as there is noise about indigenisation

no direct investment as the economy is very weak
the country`s prospects of economic recovery are bleak

a show of lack of confidence in the leadership and its policies
returns on investment against declining mental and physical capacities

Wheezy Crazy Twerking Business

They chanted and whistled with a frenzy of its own life.
Rowdy, they blocked traffic and threatened other people.

They condemned the West and the puppets and the opposition.
Marching, chanting—they shouted, 'Down with the detractors'.

Singing revolutionary songs, they wildly danced on pot-holed roads.
Their leaders arrived and chanted slogans and condemned the detractors.

After a while the leaders and supporters got into some wheezy crazy twerking business.
What a way of carrying themselves to the highest degree of ethics, self-respect and grace!

Ramshackle Bus

Troubled, the engine croaks. The smoke emitted is
rotten to the core. Will changing the driver give the
passive but chocked passengers some joy or reprieve?

Up in smoke is credibility. Up in flames is sanity.
What has safely fled is safety. The clattering
it makes is a symptom of an imminent precipice .

Like a hopeless drunk it totters. It croaks and
staggers ,disregarding red traffic lights. Trust
has all but disappeared. There is uproar.

The engine is coughing terribly. As if that were
not enough distress ,Mouse seems to be carefree.
One passenger is not flattered. She tells Mouse to halt.

Some say Mouse is drunk. Many even claim he is dog-
tired, partially deaf and blind. However, what is as bare
as a tractor driver is that the shaky bus has veered off the road!

Retirement Villages

Is their absence not somehow loud
and ear-deafening? No decent
retirement villages in Africa?

Who will write some sort of
face-saving memoirs when those
who should be are busybodies?

It is one thing to deal with
those who are agile and
innovative and have a soul.

It is another to have to contend
with soulless geriatrics who
have run out of ideas.

They are not short of a sick
proclivity to play dull antics
of backwardness and nastiness.

Dealing with the nasty mischief
of power-crazy dinosaurs is
an awkward mission and a half.

A lizard`s health hazard for they
esteem not the sanctity
of life and choice.

They sit and talk
nothing with nobody
like nobody`s business.

They fool themselves that
they are still in vogue,
yet they are in denial.

They have gone past their
sell-by date and should just
consider a date with retirement.
Where are the retirement villages
in mother Africa? Where is the fresh air?

Where is the vision? Dilapidated faces.

 Oh what do we face? Dilapidated faces!
Oh who are in the race? Dilapidated faces!
Oh rat race with dilapidated faces...faces...faces!

A Day In The Life Of Vile Violator

roundly raise your voice against injustice perpetrated against the weak
make a collective quest to promote and protect girls and women
from male and female predators or paedophiles and misogynists
stand firm with the defenceless girls and women everywhere
in the face of those who thrive on violence and bullying
those who are disgraceful and disrespectful
those who know no right or boundary
where is the full power of the law
to arrest the shenanigans
of a loose cannon?

The Lake Of Vice And Valour

the traveller marvelled at those swimming at the lake of human rights
they swam against all the odds--their gallantry too awesome to fathom
the bottomless lake was choking with corrosive dirt and inhuman odour
the shocked visitor caught sight of kidnapping snakes and sharks of ruin
he wondered about the whereabouts of the big fish of justice and peace
and whose overall responsibility was it to ensure the safety of the divers?

Shrinking Shingle Edge

The carriers say they cannot carry the cute zollars.
How come? They must be kidding us. *Our* zollars!
Are zollars not as light as feathers? Come on, airlines.
You are better than this. Don't you for a moment
imagine how it is like to be a *zollar*. No global trips.

No little reparation or moving out of the country
to hang out with other international currencies?
Your hands are tied. You are bored. You are stuck.
They say you suck. You begin to feel like a sick alien.
Your dear countrymen deride you. Fake or f-what?

People call you names. Toilet paper. Unusable
dosh. Surrogate *sheet*. Who likes to be called
s-somethig? Put yourselves in their shoes for
a moment. Of course, they were sneaked in
through the back door. But that is how it works!

Now there is the fear of the 2008 resurrection
to deal with. Would the infamous food items fly off
the shelves again? Would *bad* airlines stay away?
Will emptiness ejaculate in the shops and banks?
Will poor cows be a medium of exchange? Stone age!

The Disillusioned Voters` Discussion

A: What kind of planet do these callous politicians come from?

B: I think it`s one of those planets where callousness is the opium.

A: Some food items lack certain vitamins, hence we need a balanced diet.
   What can you say about some of these politicians who are a liability?

B: They lack something too.

A: What is it?

B: Human features! They should go back to their planet of hard-heartedness
and one-sidedness. We need a balanced diet of politics, we`re undernourished.

A Soul In Solitude

That old ragged man lives alone in a homestead devoid of human voices
Only his occasional coughing and sneezing give the passers –by
An inkling of the presence of a soul in that secluded home

They wonder what he eats in that state of seclusion or isolation
They also fail to attribute his lack of contact with people to something
For it may stem from bad relationships or loss of loved ones or deliberate choice

Does he enjoy his loneliness? Why does he live away from everyone else?
From human interaction? They ask themselves many questions as they throw cursory glances at him
He looks at them as if reminding them that solitude is a state of being alone without being lonely.

Workshop Them

Our history must not be a story
Lost in the lies of distorters
There lies the crust
Of our fatalities

Our history must not be a treasure
Lost in the bellies of hearsay
There lies the layer
Of toxicants

Our progenies must possess
The exact accounts of our past
In order to chart out
A confident trek

Our youngsters must be re-orientated
To retrace our journeys and ways
And undo imposed indignities
Of lies and lunacies

Condemned To A Mad Monster

when she was freezing and shivering
her mind drifted down memory lane
to a time she could use her electric
heater whenever she saw it fit to
do so…not now because
the power tariffs had
simply banned her--
besides electricity
had become
an off-and –on
mad monster

Rogue Characters

A lone hunter sang as he voyaged
until he arrived in a distant country
run by predators and dictators.

The predators and dictators ordered
him to halt singing and moving ---
and then robbed him of everything.

Big Brown Begging Bowl Blown Away

She used to sing thus as she travelled:
big brown begging bowl on my head
beseech bosses to bless me with
their bits and remnants falling off
their mouths and majestic tables
for I am a scum of the earth.

The big wigs –like pigs—would strive to feast on her,
seeking to suck carnal syrupiness out of her breasts,
out of her lips and curves in spite of her poor pleas;
when she was deaf to their little lousy mewing,
they barked in their pool of self-importance,
greed and self-glorification.

One final day she sang as she scampered away:
a good man leaves an inheritance
to his children`s children, and the wealth
of the sinner is laid up for the just,
blessed are the meek.
for they shall inherit the earth.

They shall cast their silver in the streets,
and their gold shall be removed,
their silver and gold shall not be able
to deliver them in the day of the wrath
because it is the stumbling block
of their iniquity.

You rich men, weep and howl
for your miseries that shall come upon you,
your riches are corrupted,
your gold and silver is cankered;
and the rust of them shall be a witness against you,
and shall eat your flesh as it were fire.

She would no longer go about
carrying a big begging bowl
with the ample knowledge
of being a blessed heiress--
Nkosazana will shine
as the princess.

It Is Theirs, Please Do Not Ruin It Any Further

The future of Africa does not belong to obsessions with power and
    sloganeering like
"Down with the West, down with the detractors, down with this and that."
Neither does it belong to the worship of lavish lifestyles and BASHES.

When bashes are held amidst a flood of awful unemployment figures
and poverty and general suffering of the citizens, then any decent
African citizen is bound to feel offended or to raise EYEBROWS.

No amount of sloganeering and posturing and pretence
or indeed silencing or wiping away of dissenting voices
will rescue Africa from the socio-economic woes of the DAY.

The young groups are having a lot of unanswered questions:
when will African leaders nip corruption in the bud or own up
to their failures and follies and prioritise development and PEACE?

The youth want to be the game changers, the masters
of their destinies and dreams, the voices of reason--
but are leaders listening to them, giving them SPACE?

What if the youth have the gift of sight to see a better Africa, a blessed
continent whose time to become the economic and cultural powerhouse
of the world is no longer a mere wet, pipe dream- but a reality of
TOMORROW?

Are you going to give the youth the opportunity to take part in rebuilding
and reinventing Africa so that it does not remain stuck in endless wars or
    poverty
or remain vulnerable and amenable to neo-colonialist machinations and
    INSTITUTIONS?

The youth are saying if it is true *that the older we become the wiser we are*
    then why do
we still have sixty-something year old, tired, clueless and useless folk
    masquerading
as saviours and youth leaders in some African nations or presidents whose
    terms EXPIRED?

Their message, their plea, their position is as simple as "nothing is for us
    without us."
They are saying some African leaders will tell you "we have this and that for
    the youth
and the women" but when one looks at it realistically there is no funding but
    ABUSE.

It is clear that the future of Africa does not belong to the greedy geriatric
    dictators
or the dinosaurs who no longer fit in with the fast-paced realities of this world
but to the youth of substance, vision and courage, so that it moves
    FORWARD.

Sons And Daughters Of The Soil

History cannot be uprooted
like the weeds from one`s gardens.

This piece cannot sufficiently reveal
and revere all the great names and deeds
of the sons and daughters of this lovely land.

This piece cannot adequately tell
Mthwakazi`s stories of pains, paradoxes,
blatant abductions and mass killings.

But this piece wonders why injustice
has been pampered, painted and protected
as justice by powerful paragons of virtue.

For how long should people live without justice?
Is it a crime to fight for justice? How can we move
from scars to stars without justice? Who are you fooling?

One patient and peaceful man used to work
with the Gukurahundi victims and survivors—
seeking nothing but justice for the poor souls.

On the 8th of February 2012 that man
disappeared. That man was none other than
the ever-smiling, ever-patient Paul Chizuze.

This piece demands answers. For how long
should people live without justice?
Is it a crime to fight for justice? How
does a person disappear? For how long?

In the depths of their hearts sons and daughters of the soil--
--people will always cherish your gallant contributions
to the freedom, dignity and growth of our communities.
Though their tears are shrouded in mystery and suspicion.

Your noble efforts are at variance with those that have always
been incorrigible haters and oppressors in mind, body and soul.
Those who have never tolerated opposition or different views

and opinions in whatever shape or size or colour.

From outspoken legislators to writers, the nation salutes you.
From patriotic economists and commentators--like Eric Block--
the citizens are indeed poorer after their departure.

Payne Arnold , you are a true son of the soil for you pushed a 210 litre drum
of water from Victoria Falls to Gwanda (over 500kms) and emptied the 210
litres of Zambezi water in Gwanda.
You were willing and committed.
You didn't want to see people
continuously drown in water woes.

In his emotionally-charged speech at the funeral of a fearless
freedom fighter and commander, Dr Joshua Nkomo said:
"Those who rule our country know inside themselves that
Lookout played a very big part in winning our struggle.
And yet they let him die in prison. I say he died in prison
because he died on that bed on which he was detained.
It was not possible for him to leave that bed and it was
not possible for you to see him.

Therefore, I say he died in prison. Why should men
like Lookout and Dumiso, after being found innocent
of any wrongdoing by the highest court in this land
remain detained? When we ask we get the same answer
from the Minister as we used to get from the Smith regime.
Mafela, Lookout, after all his sacrifices, died a pauper in our own hands.
We cannot blame colonialism and imperialism for this tragedy.

We who fought against these things now practise them.
Why? Why? Why? We are enveloped in the politics of hate.
The amount of hate that is being preached today
in this country is frightful."

He stressed that what the country fought for was peace,
progress, love, respect, justice, equality, not the opposite.
He bemoaned corruption as one of the worst evils bleeding the country.

 He did not mince his words in describing you, Lookout
"Mafela" Khalisabantu Vumindaba Masuku as a hero who fought
against fascism, oppression, tribalism and corruption. He added,
"Any failure to dedicate ourselves to the ideals of Masuku will be

a betrayal of him and of all those freedom fighters whose graves
are not known. Our country cannot progress on fear and false accusations
which are founded simply on the love of power".

Possibly the most popular singer to come out of Bulawayo, Majee,,
as Lovemore "Majaivana" Tshuma was affectionately called, was
a musical marvel whose songs reverberated across the whole country.
His songs were pregnant with meaning, relatable and politically prophetic.
In 2000 he left the country for the USA like most of the nation`s citizens who
sought a better life in the diaspora, and little did his legion of fans think that
he had he hung the microphone for good. It was simply inconceivable.
Years later, his diehard fans decided to petition him on Facebook, hoping to
galvanise him out of a lengthy retirement, but their efforts were unheeded.
As one listens to his timeless music on various radios one hopes that one day
one would wake up to see Matabeleland`s music icon perform at Emagumeni.

Tribute to the late but great president of Imbovane Yamahlabezulu,
Bekithemba Sibindi .He was a fearless leader and academic whose vibrant
pressure group held ground-breaking and well-attended discussions and
debates on human rights and development. The group sought to lobby the
United Nations to open a commission of enquiry into the Matabeleland
massacres.
The group used to present platforms at which disgruntled and frustrated
citizens found outlets to vent their anger and grievances. Through such
educative ,frank and therapeutic interactions, attendees` fears were
demystified in spite of the high-handedness and callousness of the former
president`s spy agents and their overzealous sympathizers.

Homage to Mqondisi Moyo the founding member and current President
of Mthwakazi Republic Party. No stranger to abuse and threats from
government, the maverick leader and his party are a tireless hands-on
team that is redefining the political landscape as they battle against
critical and current socio-economic challenges bedevilling the locals
in a manner that has baffled their opponents and endeared them to
several people both within and without the boundaries of the country
and the continent. They are keeping the unrepentant government`s
policemen on their toes as they respond to the locals` distress calls
without hesitation. They stand out as practical problem- solvers.

He once declared "I am a survivor of the Gukurahundi atrocities.
I witnessed my parents and neighbours being beaten up. I believe
that art can be used to expose human rights violations and atrocities

that have taken place in Zimbabwe". Those were the words of Owen Maseko, a prominent and respected visual artist and installation artist whose gallant Gukurahundi paintings saw him being arrested on charges of "undermining the authority of the president". Titled Sibathontisele which is IsiNdebele for *Let's DripOn Them*, his exhibition highlighted brutal and bloody nature of the Gukurahundi atrocities.

David Coltart is a well-known human rights advocate, a former Member of Parliament for Bulawayo South in the House of Assembly, a former Minister for Education, Sport, Arts and Culture and a founder of a Legal Advice Centre in Bulawayo who has been working untiringly to uplift the lives of the ordinary people. He established the Bulawayo Legal Projects Centre, a legal aid clinic which has played an instrumental role in make sure the poor citizens access legal advice and representation.

Firebrand, Paul Siwela is a leader of Matabeleland Liberation Organisation (MLO) who was persecuted by the former president for seeking justice for the marginalized groups and provinces of Matabeleland and the Midlands. Tribute to former and current Presidents of Mthwakazi Liberation Front (MLF) General Nandi Nandi and Dr Churchill Guduza respectively. The 1893 Mthwakazi Human Rights Restoration Movement has been on the forefront of spearheading human rights issues.

In January 2018 Ibhetshu LikaZulu secretary-general Mbuso Fuzwayo, Dumisani Mpofu of Masakhaneni Trust, Charles Thomas, a victim of Gukurahundi sued former president ,incumbent president, the vice-president and British Premier demanding release of the findings of the Chihambakwe Commission of Inquiry on the Gukurahundi massacres. Mr. Mbuso Fuzwayo has been unequivocal on the forefront of preserving and advancing people`s history and culture. He is the voice of the people which lambasts an arrogant culture of importing or imposing leaders from other regions.

When MDC Matabeleland South provincial chairperson Pilate Ndebele walked into Bulawayo Central Police Station in February 2018 his intention was clear, to open a docket against the former president so that he could be arrested for the Gukurahundi crimes against humanity. When the police refused the heroic activist threatened to stage a lone protest . He told Southern Eye "They also asked if I had any evidence about Mugabe's involvement in Gukurahundi,and I told them other than the several mass graves in Matabeleland, his admission that it was a moment of madness was evidence enough."

Born in Plumtreen, Jason Ziyaphapha Moyo was Zapu`s Vice-President, and a founder of the Zimbabwe People's Revolutionary Army. A hero, Rodgers Alfred Nikita Mangena, was the commander of the Zimbabwe People's Revolutionary Army. Described as inconsistent by Zanu PF's supreme decision-making body, and not accorded heroine status Thenjiwe Lesabe`s death brew a political and tribal storm Angered Zapu members and locals described her as an undisputed heroine and gave her a huge send off at her farm. They slammed Zanu-PF for victimizing corpses and disrespecting the dead. She was not buried at the National Heroes Acre because Zanu PF saw it fit not to award her heroine status as she had defected to the revived Zapu . Zapu threatened to exhume remains of its liberation heroes from the national shrine. The Zapu Council of Elders chairperson and the struggle heroine`s burial was attended by ANC chairperson, Baleka Mbete.

If Zimbabwe had just 50 % or more of citizens with her kind of gusto, standpoint and ideals on issues of equality, possibly, if not definitely , the country would much united, with women and different individuals and tribes being valued equally. Her name is Priscilla Misihairabwi-Mushonga, an outspoken human rights activist and feminist, a former Member of the National Assembly for Umzingwane Constituency,
She has not only ardently advanced for the creation of opportunities for women, spoke out against the abuse of women, public institutions and funds, corruption, also she has condemned domination of one tribe in parliament, government, business and other other spheres. Speaking on a radio on 28th July 2018 she said, 'The problem is not Shona people but Shona hegemony". Citing issues of marginalisation she spearheaded what they termed "the Matabeleland Agenda" which was a drive to focus on devolution, women`s sexual and reproductive rights and other regional challenges. Fluent in both Ndebele and Shona, and born to a Shona father, she is certainly one of the few and fearless voices that have continued to query why it is acceptable to debate issues in Shona in the august House but when someone seeks to do the same in Ndebele, they are told to switch to a "language" everybody understands as if Ndebele is not one of the official languages in the country. A defiant legislator, a Co-Founder and Coordinator of Women And AIDS Support Network, a founding member of the National Constitutional Assembly, she is considered as a voice of the voiceless and a heroine in Matabeleland.

It was an open secret that almost of all the cabinet members hand-picked from Matabeleland by the former president were his dangerous and trusted hero-

worshippers. When Priscilla was the Regional Integration and International Co-operation Minister, she once slammed politicians in Matabeleland, and called them 'useless condoms' who had sold out the region. In 2014 she called the wife of the deposed president," "Pawn star in Zanu PF politics'. Known for sometimes adopting such unorthodox and radical ways as bringing babies, panties and pads in parliament to highlight issues close to her heart , in January 2018 Priscilla brought menstrual cups and tampons into the National Assembly to illuminate the need for the provision of free sanitary wear for girls . In June 2018, she torched a media frenzy when she filed nomination papers on behalf of former MDC president Dr Thokozane Khupe, wearing a red T-shirt adorned "Hure"at the back and "Me Too" in front in protest against Nelson Chamisa`s supporters who had hounded and shouted Hure to Dr Khupe at the Supreme Court in Harare.
"Hure" is a Shona term for harlot. Dr Khupe is the President of the MDC-T whilst Nelson Chamisa is the current MDC Alliance President.

Pricilla swore that she would wear the "Hure" T-shirt, saying an injury to one woman was an injury to all. She once carried used panties to parliament to push for the prohibition of the sale of used underwear. On who women should vote for, she said: "When you are gripped by a demon that wants you to vote for a man, lift up your skirts and check your bottom and then you will know who to vote for." A widow herself, contributing on the topic: "Are Women Being Marginalised" she told the wife of the late general and the former vice president that as long as she is still attractive she will date any man she has feelings for. "Date, have somebody and have pretty good sex with someone, because men are doing it every other day, who says we have to be angels? We have to be in a nunnery, "she stated.

A recipient of several international accolades and awards including the Law Society of England and Wales Humans Rights of the Year Award, International Woman of Courage Award and the American Bar Association International Human Rights Award, Beatrice Mtetwa has been named one of the bravest lawyers in Africa and is globally admired for her unwavering courage in fighting for human rights and free speech in Zimbabwe. She was embraced by the former US First Lady Michelle Obama when she became the 2014 International Women of Courage Awardee at the 2014 Secretary of State's International Women of Courage Award Ceremony at the U.S. Upon receiving an ULaw Honorary Doctorate 2015, she said, "My motivation really comes from the fact that people's rights continued to be trampled upon and as most of these are rights protected under the country's laws, I feel it is my duty to continue highlighting the fact that these rights were given so that they could be enjoyed and where violations occur, I try to do all I can to preserve these rights and their enjoyment".

Mtetwa, considered as the nation's top human rights lawyer, was the first person to be honoured with both The Burton Benjamin Memorial Award and the Committee to Protect Journalists' International Press Freedom Award. The only African besides Nelson Mandela to receive the Ludovic-Trarieux International Human Rights Prize from France, her first job was prosecuting cases for the new government of the first black president, but job disillusioned with the "selective justice" she eventually decided to open her own law firm with a view to representing respondents victimized by the oppressive regime. Living in a country where the law is repeatedly used as a weapon of persecution, she has defended those beleaguered victims, at great personal risk.

Described by the Guardian in 2009 as "one of the most troublesome thorns in Mugabe's side", Jenni Williams is one of the Women of Zimbabwe Arise's heroic leaders who by August 2016
had been arrested over 65 times. Asked on what led to the formation of WOZA, she explained, "Women, individuals, some from church women's wings, gathered together in 2002 to talk about the bad governance, economic meltdown and the culture of fear caused by Posa Public Order and Security Act and Aippa Access to Information and Protection of Privacy Act. They decided rather than to suffer in silence as was done during Gukurahundi, they would speak truth to power, be visible through peaceful protests as a way of showing Zimbabweans how to hold political leadership accountable for the crisis." Born in Gwanda, Matabeleland South , Williams is a recipient of the International Women of Courage Award and Robert F. Kennedy Human Rights Award. Fearless, the pro-democracy campaigner

Therefore, to all the living and fallen heroes and heroines of the soil, your ideals must and will not remain in limbo forever. You are the royal sons and daughters of Mzilikazi. You are the sons and daughters of the soil.
The people will speak…

*The distance between the Victoria Falls and the town of Gwanda is over 500 km
Lala ngoxolo means "Rest in eternal peace"".
Ubuqhawe bakho kabuthandabuzwa means "Your level of heroism is unquestionable"".

Immortal

You have departed
but your words continue to
give us wisdom and entertainment.

You have gone beyond
but your words are immortal,
they speak now and to future generations.

You had your neologisms,
Mthandazo Ndema Ngwenya,
those rare amalgams for socio-cultural terminology

You were on song,
Mayford Sibanda, you died young;
you produced some of the most outstanding pieces.

Who shall talk about nationhood?
Who shall ask pertinent questions
about a people's cultural pride?

Who?
Who shall talk and walk the talk?
And walk towards renewal and resurrection of confidence?

Prolific, pragmatic and progressive,
Ndebezinhle S. Sigogo produced classics
like Akulazulu eMhlabeni.[1]

Affectionately known as BD,
Bernard D. Ndlovu was a creative novelist and poet.
Humble, he helped aspiring writers hone their skills.

Chinua Achebe
is an African literary lion who roared through Things Fall Apart
and shaped and shook modern African literature.

---

[1] *Akulazulu eMhlabeni is in SiNdebele. It means, "There is no Heaven on Earth."*

African authors,
please continue to tell your story
without any shred of fear or favour.

Wonders Will Never Cease

That group stunned the citizens
with their home-grown optimism
and Mickey Mouse verbal aerobatics.
They harped on instant prosperity
propelled by their great discovery.
People pinched their bodies upon
hearing the optimists' story of refined
diesel streaming mystifyingly out of rocks!
Now there is a prosperous multi-currency system
after the wondrous departure of the national money!

Keep Off!

We keep our roads
    we keep our reptiles
    we even keep our animals

Dereliction paints the
    surfaces of the national
    roads with potholes that
    all-in giraffes can transform
    into some kind of domicile

Be in cricket or tennis or golf
    we demand indigenisation
     Africa is for Africans!
    Don't they know that?

There is fear that the abrupt inclusion
    of black players into national
    teams is not based on merit
    but cronyism, hence cricket
    is now chaotic as the world rankings
    bear testimony to political mingling
    some circles have accused the
    government of double standards
    and of practising regionalism
    tribalism and reverse racism
    where they berate whites for
    lack of patriotism on one hand
    (they hardly attend 'national`
    events, like the independence
    or heroes day or other juicy galas)
    on the other hand they host world
    class white sportspersons in
    lavish presidential residences as
    queens and kings who give
    the country international pride

Let those who say the transport
    system has collapsed by virtue
    of fuel shortages take a nap
    on the roads!

Damning reports of casualties
　　have not stirred the minister
　　of roads to resurface or widen
　　the roads which kombis and
　　buses jangle on daily
　　one war vet has stunned the
　　protesting commuters by
　　telling them what bloody
　　counter-revolutionary irritants
　　or tea-boys of the West they are--
　　proudly he claims he died
　　in the bush for the country!

Lies! Lies! Lies!
　　all the same the land reform
　　will go on
　　we're revolutionaries(a fist
　　in ferocious wavering)
　　they rush to their masters
　　don't listen to our detractors
　　apologists of the West
　　and stooges of the West
　　we will crash them
　　our war credentials are perfect
　　we have solid support from our
　　brothers and sisters even
　　in America(the national
　　TV runs a hyped footage
　of a presidential hero's
　welcome by Harlem residents)
　　we're impeccable
　　we will build on our
　　series of successes
　　all the arms of
　　government are raring
　　to go

Some commentators are saying
　　by the way things are turning out
　　the land reform
　　is set to be a huge 'land deform'
　　yet claims of a series of successes

are a mirage save for successes
in impoverishing and oppressing
the populace
a number of newspaper analysts
concur that no sane black
American will support oppressive
African leaders, let alone pray
To be ruled by them after centuries
of racism and slavery
they say the Harlem meeting
was one propaganda tool and hoax
stage-managed and used by poor
overzealous blacks accused of various
crimes in cahoots with their ruling black
elitists from Africa who seek to be shored
up by hook and crook since their ship
is sinking because of bungling
and international unpopularity

People shouldn't be worried
we're building more power
stations and upgrading our
systems countrywide
as a landlocked country
we're our importing electricity
from neighbouring countries

Power outages are a pain in
the lives of individuals
and institutions
with residents going without
electricity for more than
two days per week
and companies hard-hit by
power-induced idleness
job losses are horrifying
the country is saddled
with chronic power
problems which have
rendered leaders useless
totally clueless

The reports and tears of
    the commuters fall on
    the back of a duck whose
    wings are in limbo with
    one leg in the grave
    one Nkayi woman once
    warned the kombi and
    bus drivers: over a period
    of swaying and swinging
    up and down
    they risk being barren or
    buttock- less!

Another man once said:
    if a doctor gives you a
    bottle of medicine with
    instructions to shake well
    before drinking
    swig the solution and take
    a bumpy ride and the trick
    would be done!

No matter what the alarmists
    and prophets of doom say:
    no single person will die of
    hunger in this land of honey
    cholera is a biological warfare
    unleashed by our jealous
    former colonizers
    let this sink into their heads:
    we will never ever be a
    colony again!

Military escapades and
    disproportionate defence
    portifolo expenditure have
    been condemned by citizens
    and observers alike
    including a bloated cabinet
    and high level corruption
    and cronyism
    more than ninety per cent of

the population will need food
aid and cholera has reached
continues to be a menace
in Mashonaland

Keep your Britain
    I will keep my country!
    (yet some sycophantic
    voice was once heard chant:
    the Blair l know is a toilet!)
    l have but one God
   He is in Heaven!
    my people…my people
    the health sector will
    be boosted in a big way
    more clinics and hospitals
    will be built for you
    no single child will die
    because of lack
    of medical attention
    indigenisation of the farms
    and firms is going on smoothly
    unemployment levels are set
    to drop and drop drastically
    as sons and daughters of the soil
    we're taking back what rightfully
    belongs to us in this land of honey
    and milk… and so that's that
    it`s a fast-track exercise
    we are taking back our
    companies… and next…
    our mines will be nationalised

Reports of flawed tender
    systems with serious
    allegations of unbridled cases
    of nepotism, tribalism and
    reverse racism have been
    downplayed by government
    officials and party spin-doctors
    they are adamant and upbeat
    however economists have

warned government on company
closures and farm seizures
it is clear government officials
are globe-trotting and seeking
medical attention overseas

War vets are on the forefront of taking
back the land which they say the
former colonisers stole and did not
even pay a mere cent for

Some critical observers contend that while
equitable land redistribution is an
unavoidable issue, they doubt the
capabilities of some war vets in
utilizing prime land, as some of them
once made exorbitant disability
claims which indicated that they were
literally beyond 90% disabled
They warn that it will take a huge
miracle for such untrained invalids
to work the land productively for
domestic needs and export

We say no to interference
in our internal affairs
we are a sovereign state
we run our elections
we manage our resources
why does the opposition
always run to the West?

Puppets! Puppets of the West!

There is rampant looting of the country's
minerals with cronies and government
officials being implicated in several
scandals and commissions of inquiry
whose reports are an exercise in futility

We taught them democracy
let them go to hell
we will never ever be a
colony again!

Demonstrators have been
   severely beaten up
   writers and journalists
   have been persecuted
   more and more dissenting
   people are haunted or jailed
   some have been abducted
   the human rights groups
   have called on government
   to act on these abductions
   and disappearances, noting
   with concern that there has
   been a steady a trend
   on the part of government
   to sweep such abuses
   under the carpet

Our people love and support us
   in spite of all the lies peddled
   by the opposition and their
   Western sponsors and puppets
   we will have a landslide victory

Before the election people are forced
   to attend day and night meetings
   and warned by the militias of the
   consequences of not voting for
   certain individuals and the
   'people's party' with war credentials
   campaigns are marked by violent
   attacks on and senseless deaths
   of opposition members
   vote-buying ad rigging and
   intimidation of voters are said
   to be the order of the day

We fought and this is a party of blood
   this country was unchained by blood
   let no- one fool themselves
   we fought for this nation
   losers should just accept defeat
   we don't know them and why do

they want to vote?
my people are here in our land
why would people choose to do
menial jobs in far-away lands ?

Those in the Diaspora cry foul
because they are denied the right
to vote through a postal system
they are known to demonstrate each
time the officials visit their countries
of refuge or permanent residence
villagers say some chiefs are no longer
genuine traditional leaders but agents
of oppression and intimidation
because of the electrified and
beautiful houses built by 'government'
and the cars they were pampered
with so that they could become
blind and selfish and soulless

There is no crisis here
what crisis? this is their strategy for
what they call regime change!
never ever! our people will decide!
the arms of government are
functioning well and independently
we call for the removal of sanctions
the country will have a bumper
harvest this year
they raise eyebrows about
the food situation or the death of
one single white farmer!
last year we had a severe drought
how many blacks ,especially
poor and underpaid farm workers
have died because of white brutality,
and without an outcry from their kin
and kith? we are fast-tracking the land
(Australia is a country of thieves!)
public servants must be submissive
we pay their salaries
they have to show loyalty

it's that simple or else they quit

Judiciary rulings have been upturned
   cronies are stampeding for several
   farm and company ownerships
   while party hooligans are reportedly
   chasing away and brutalising white
   farmers who have vowed to stay put
   (some farmers have died in cold blood
   and Matabeleland residents have been
   threatened with another obnoxious
   dose of Gukurahundi) for stating that
  the government is behind the invasion
  of their villages and farms by outsiders

   some prime farms have been vandalized
   chunks and chunks of seized land
   lie idle as those who are supposed
   to farm are busy gyrating madly on the
   fields, and this a common feature
   of national programmes on TV and
   radio touted as agricultural activities!
   the government vehemently
   denies that it is squarely responsible for
   the poor yields and chaos on the farms
   yet other countries in the same region
   have registered surplus food reserves
   economic meltdown is severely taking
   its toll as villagers are said to have
   resorted to eating tree roots for survival
   whilst more and more companies
   and farms have become
   nothing but a white elephant
   the police have said people who
   complain or form groups for no
   clear reasons will be arrested
   the people have spoken through
   the ballot in a free and fair fashion
   and hence those who break the
   laws of the land will be brought
   to book with zero tolerance!

Our schools are the best in the world
        standards have not fallen that low
        it's a lie that the education sector
        is a pale shadow of the 1980s system
        we have localized our 'O' examinations
        the cabinet consists of highly educated
        individuals, even the British one is no
        match for or patch on his one!
        we have no reason to shop overseas
        these bans serve to hurt our citizens
        to hell with aid if it is conditional!

Because of alarming human rights
        record the party officials and their
        cronies have been internationally
        slammed and named and shamed
        they have been slapped with travel
        embargoes
        but they are raving and ranting
        about such a ban in spite of their
        avowed abhorrence for decadent
        Western lifestyles and policies
        apparently owing to cravings for
        great overseas shopping sprees
        most of their children are being
        educated in the West anyway

        Once a beacon of education and food
        the country has become a
        pitiful pariah state of anarchy…

Nyaope-Ruled

"That's utter rubbish!" she wrote.
The limping athlete had *won* the race.

The article writer described the athlete
as someone who enjoyed *popular success*--

even warning people that he was set to *win*
in the future *with or without limbs and eye*s.

The gimpy runner was known for his love
of luxury. He had a fleet of poshy cars.

He threw lavish party after lavish party.
Did he have a modicum of care in this world?

If some people thought that he was wasteful,
was he wasting anybody's money or his?

When did it become a crime to spoil
oneself with fun, with overseas trips and all?

People always whispered that he had *cruel* villas
and stashes of *sick* money in far foreign lands.

It was common knowledge that the athlete
did not only train outside for major contests

he also frequented better-equipped health centres
and hotels whenever he fell sick or had a craving.

Were people jealous of the sprinter's lifestyle?
Was it their business what he bought or ate

or what kind of medical care he received?
Was it at their cost? Yes, at all costs he flew out!

Was it their right to know what he was up
to whenever he flew in or out?

If he preferred better managed, funded
and equipped facilities, what was amiss?

If he decided whimsically or otherwise—to fly out
and have fun or a check-up, what was wrong?

Did he have to remind them it was his money--
and that he owed no citizen a life or an explanation?

Was it their business that by a stroke
of miracle he had romped to victory *again*?

Yes *again*. Well, if he did not flout rules,
why was there so much hullabaloo here?

One Facebooker agreed with True,
the lady who wrote: *utter rubbish*.

The unemployed youth read the article
with his critical mind and commented,

"Either you are high on a killer drug
like **whoonga** or you suffer terribly

from psychotic episodes and delusions.
Look for the nearest asylum urgently".

** nyaope or whoonga or wunga ---a highly addictive street drug widely available in South
Africa
mbanje, SiNdebele for marijuana*

Ramshackle Bus

Troubled, the engine croaks. The smoke emitted is
rotten to the core. Will changing the driver give the
passive but chocked passengers some joy or reprieve?

Up in smoke is credibility. Up in flames is sanity.
What has safely fled is safety. The clattering
it makes is a symptom of an imminent precipice .

Like a hopeless drunk it totters. It croaks and
staggers ,disregarding red traffic lights. Trust
has all but disappeared. There is uproar.

The engine is coughing terribly. As if that were
not enough distress ,Mouse seems to be carefree.
One passenger is not flattered. She tells Mouse to halt.

Some say Mouse is drunk. Many even claim he is dog-
tired, partially deaf and blind. However, what is as bare
as a tractor driver is that the shaky bus has veered off the road!

Firming It Up

failed in fairness
fielded in polls
to cement it all
a family's favour
a dynastic chair

Not Working

when one thought it couldn't
get any worse, the destroyers
are upping their game

this drama has gone astray
it is not getting any better
but the better of liberties

this crowd has to be tagged
its acts simply hash-tagged
use the words: out of order

causalities are human rights
stateless are the vulnerable
reason and decency impugned

from downstairs to upstairs
there is some silly shakiness
please use one word: madness

peace and order vilified
rules and ethics denigrated
the nation misses comfort

The State Of Affairs

beneficiaries hold it in high esteem
the greasing of palms is their scheme

ethical abortion is a daily cruel blow
either the authorities like it or are slow

people who screw and suck others dry
are content with the status quo`s sigh

do the powers see that the existing order
of things is nothing else but disorder?

why amass a wealth of educational papers
only to become little law-abiding paupers?

be sleek and swim in sharks' shady dealings
and you will live in gold-and -silver dwellings

but remember that when order finally knocks
there will be some serious gnashing of padlocks!

Willowy Words

The man with a sprinkling hair in the head said,
"You can have a coconut-oiled hair or
a lotioned body that glimmers like a star,
but if you don't wash your body thoroughly
you are as good as a rancid food eater who thinks
his mouth and tummy are the refuge for freshness".

Unswayed Folly

a tortoise
has a clownish tendency
of farting and urinating
and sleeping and defecating
on the heads of those who
keep it for whatever reason

when people lie and claim
they're unable to be affected
by dung and damage or unaffected
by bigotry or untouched by suffocating odour
or immune to indecency or impervious to thuggery
then all this begets a big question: are they real?

Submerged Voices

cultural and artistic spaces
violated

artistic freedom under threat
imprisoned

voices of reason trampled
drowned

brutal and macabre hands
raised

Students Are Studying Starvation Out There

the parents are up in arms against chaps
who come up with overseas scholarships

which are not sustainably financed or supported
therefore pushing poor students into a big den

of privation which in turn gives birth to prostitution
if people don't have capacity why claim and commit?

the tentacles of government paralysis are being felt everywhere
the odour of economic non-functionality is evidently pervasive!

Authenticity Gives Birth To Capacity

There, under a Mopani tree
The young man sat –alone
He started a conversation--
A hard talk with his inner self

We all know it though sometimes
We may not necessarily touch or see it
It is found in existentialist philosophy
It can manifest itself in aesthetics too

We call some artists 100 % authentic
Does it mean that others are inadequate?
Are they fake, resentful of their personality?
Are they victims of external pressures or what?

If people disown their hearts and innate freedom
And adopt false values because of money and all
Can they excel in careers driven by self-deception?
Shouldn't they be true to their personality at all costs?

Drowning Citizens

Dear floating and fooling kings and queens,
Can you hear desperate distant shrieks?
"I'm drowning! I'm drowning!"

Weak as he is, he walked all the way,
Listen to this patient from the hospital,
"I'm still in pain. No painkillers. No food".

The councillor is overwhelmed,
Each month pools and pools balloon,
Rent blues and electricity bills and school fees.

The MP says the roof has simply fallen apart,
"I witness piteous things and horrendous developments,
Houses being sold, without electricity, with crying school children".

The Investigator And The Footprints

Mrs Maphosa woke up in the morning
to find her car`s rear wheels gone.

She rushed to the nearest police
station and reported the theft.

Two weeks later one police
officer pitched up.

"Madam, where are the footprints?"
quizzed the officer.

Like great author Mbulelo Mzamane,
She seldom entertained silly questions.

As she walked away, the police asked,
"Are you serous there was a theft here?"

Acute Coughs Versus A Cute Promise

When he stepped on the podium
He did not mince his words at all

He told them that he was an antidote
To their turbulent lives in the country

He couldn't finish his speech--for people`s
Thunderous severe coughs drowned it out

Money Blues Again

These monsters have resurfaced again
and penniless souls are sleeping in the cold
hoping to get their money in any currency.

When these go viral and zigzag like deadly snakes
all over pavements and on the dusty and dirty
streets, I will remind silly sullen Stonevoter

that voting for stones and Stone Age policies
brings neither joy nor development but misery
like bank queues all over the decrepit city centre.

This is what you get when you campaign day and night,
 every five years, for Stone Age policies and recycled lies
and naked poverty and robed poverty of ideas and life.

How could he expect to crack life or humanity out of a stone?
Who could have convinced him that a stone—no matter how shiny--
has neither a heart nor human elements like sympathy or empathy?

I don`t seek to be mean or unsympathetic or unfeeling like a stone—
but if Stonevoter comes again begging for money or assistance or—
silly as he is—my vote—I swear I will drill brains into his berserk brick!

There Are Times When Rituals Are Drunk

sometimes in winter a little bolt of heatwave
just springs up and wakes up the dead and dull
at times seasons come with unseasonal smirks

from time to time nightfall is a peep of dusk and dawn
at times an ant shakes up a drunk elephant into sobriety
there are times when smallness is bigger than any blaze

Hopeful People

In a future of hope
no one should enforce
upon the people a lifestyle
that lulls them into a state
of servitude and denigration.

In a better future the dishonesty and insult
of arresting those who steal with ring leaders--
whilst protecting the same infamous ring leaders
and their so-called legacy should be stamped out.

Sleeping Rivers

Sleeping rivers keep secret what they harbour,
hide their fury's strength behind a placid face

Under their tongue lies an innocence, an obedience
that catches and cripples strongmen`s tentacles

Sleeping rivers can drown the dross of dancing sharks
and unleash and flex muscles with an amazing depth

The waters of sleeping rivers—when stirred up—when
tampered with—breathe a fire which swallows up sharks

Rising To The Challenges Of Today

History is a story of now,
a story of today's activities
that becomes a story of the past.

History is not only a story of sorrow,
but a carefully-crafted story of tomorrow--
a story of what to initiate, swallow or follow.

History is a drawing shaped
by people's decisions and actions--
usually bold, boring but big and beautiful.

History is a victim's fight to claim a future,
it is an aggrieved people's stride to a destiny
through a clearly defined collective and active voice.

History is yesterday's atmospheric pressure
playing out through today's barometers of life.
History is more than a story—it is an awakening

History is not a passive past,
but a present progressive response
to the challenges of today and tomorrow.

It is our upset tummies crying out day and night
for nothing short of the detoxification and protection
of our bodies from yesterday and today's abdicables.

History is you and I doing something
about our present and future situations,
making life-changing decisions and actions.

Therefore, be brave, be ready because history
is certainly coming for and counting on you.
Today's actions are tomorrow's light or shadow.

At Long Last

People were singing and running about on the streets.
They were celebrating their victory over an obstinate tick.

Who could have imagined such a greedy and sticky
tick could be kicked off the privates of their cows and sheep?

They were sending a clear message to all the bugs and ticks
on the African continent that it was time to shape up or ship out.

It is not easy to see why—you know horse-flies and the like are bad.
These are a nightmare for humans because they make life outdoors rough.

They have a bad feeding habit of transferring blood-borne diseases
from one animal to another—besides of course, torturing their victims.

Africa has wonderful grazing pastures but our beasts are starving and weak.
These modern bugs—with their families and fans and friends-are draining our
cows.

Our beasts are haemorrhaged to death every day by these unkind and bloody
suckers.
One thing that drives people crazy is that the bugs do not accept blame for
their mess.

A Clumsy Flimsy Flip-flop

That obstinate tick, that ectoparasite has made a u-turn,
it says the backsides of mammals are too sweet to let go of.

It claims it has the inalienable right to the tender parts of birds,
to feed on the blood of helpless reptiles and amphibians—forever.

Is there justice in this world, on this beautiful African continent--
when ticks do as they wish even if they were fairly rejected?

Before the tick's shameless u-turn, some people threatened
too early, they forgot they were dealing with a heartless mite.

They sang too loudly songs of justice like a careless hunter
who frightens away the very animal he wants to catch.

It was as if they were confiding a secret to an unworthy person,
and that is as good as carrying grain in a bag with a hole.

Where were the advisers? There is a Gambian proverb that says:
a fly that has no one to advise it, follows the corpse into the grave.

Maybe they were celebrating with the idea that since the tick
had been rejected and had accepted that rejection, it was a new creature.

Why did they forget that timeless Gambian saying that says: *no matter
how long a log may float in the water, it will never become a crocodile?*

What will happen? How will they claim their blood back when a Gambian
proverb says: *if a donkey kicks you and you kick back, you are both donkeys?*

Pardoned Prisoner's Shattered Expectations

A jailbird, he had been sentenced to 30 years
 in prison, but after serving 10 years,
and in poor health ,Freddy was freed
under a presidential amnesty.

As he hobbled home-- a pale shadow of a robust man
whose reign of terror and debauchery was enshrined
 in the victims` memories--thoughts of making up
to his wife were central to his happiness.

He was imagining himself as an innocence of love,
a baby waiting for a nipple to be properly positioned,
ready to feed. Peristalsis. Away from jail`s paralysis. Away.
Experiencing. Feeling the magic, the wave-like motion. Away.

Some people on the small bus witnessed it. The movement
of his lips. Suckling. His Adam`s apple was vibrating. Dancing.
When he finally got home he witnessed a true process. A baby
involved in a process of tongue, jaw, lips and palate. Innocence.

Startled, he watched the waves of compression by the baby`s tongue
sail, move along the underside of his wife`s nipple before pushing it--
with a patent hunger--against the hard palate. The wife greeted him.
He roared, "Who`s the father of that child? " There was a loud silence.

There Is Method To Her Madness

"Does this bring food to my little table?
How many times should I tell villagers here
I no longer want to hear about that name?
Do you want my granddaughters and sons
who are sweating it out in foreign lands
to starve me after getting wind that I am
attending useless meetings arranged
by the same crazy and clueless fellows
who ran everything down and as if that
were enough damage-- chased good
citizens through violence and hunger?
Look at you: unemployed, starving
and coming here with: *Gogo, there`s
a meeting*. What! Wake up. You
want me to vomit? Get out, out!!!"

Granny MaSuku`s stick landed
hard and severally on an image
emblazoned on the front
of the visitor`s worn-out shirt.
The visitor was sent packing.
That incident sent the village
wagging tongues. Some people
said it was because of senility
or madness or both . All agreed
that whatever it was there was
a message and a method in it.

Wet And Wicked

Heavy dew lay on his lips
It was a glorious experience

Power glistened with dew
Departure wasn't overdue

Out of the question, it was taboo
His muscles were wet with dew

He was a scorer, he never missed
He was slippery , he got stuck in here

Heavy honey dripped and dripped
He didn't want to see it slip off

Though his spiky hands dripped
With the blood of innocent victims

Grab the sun too, it shouldn't set
But one day the sun had other ideas

It went down and disappeared fast
Like the morning coat on the grass

Bring Back Our History and Heritage

You have muddied the waters of
Our glorious history and heritage
Where shall we hide our long tails?
Our nakedness is now a public feast

Nurses working without their tools
Nurses and doctors exposed to diseases
Why punish them for demanding their dues?

Still Going Strong

The younger international teachers wondered
When the new teacher was introduced to them

Was she not an ailing and incontinent woman?
Was she not a has-been, a technological fossil?

Talk of a 64 year-old KiSwahili Language Teacher
Guess what: there was a peppy and practical soul!

She used the smart board and her laptop just fine
Not to mention how interactive her lessons were

There was dynamism, not technological dinosaurism
 Her techno- savviness got students eating out of her hand!

When the younger teachers` heads ran out of steam
They could count on her to recharge their flat batteries!

When the younger educators needed first aid or a tool
They did not need to look any further than her for all that

Coming from different credos, cultures and countries—
Teachers at times argued and threatened but she conciliated

First words in Swahili

English	Swahili
Welcome	Karibu
Hello	Habari
Goodbye	Kwaheri
Good morning	Habari ya asubuhi
Good afternoon	Habari ya mchana
Thank you	Asante
Sorry	Pole
Please	Tafadhali
Yes	Ndio
No	Hapana
Come here	Njoo hapa
Well done	Vizuri sana

A Lesson On How Not To Betray Oneself

he was no such a man who could bring
a moral credit upon himself by accepting
reality and the dynamics and rules of life

he was ever-ready for the harsh and crazy
political roller coaster rides yet the fragility
of his body betrayed any credibility and ability

Faces of Shamelessness

After years and years
in cabinet, after decades
and decades of lying and looting,
they cried and people responded.

They said they were now in the cold,
having hit hard times, short of money—
but people asked: why don`t you queue
for cash like us, and where`s your loot?

They said spare us your bitching: did you not
call us names, cry-babies—and what-have- you
for the past 36 years when we complained
that you had turned the country into a living hell?

A Wiggling Car

Like some computer technicians and addicts—
Changing computer parts while the computer was still running—
From a little distance the two souls in the car were both driving!

Like some passionate presenters and orators----
Giving a talk without preparing or time to rehearse—
The couple was improvising, focusing: winging it in style!

Some onlookers undoubtedly shook their heads in dismay
Yet others, for their part in foolery, giggled giddily with glee
On the fly, the two, the car inched and wriggled like a worm!

Marvellous` Marvellous Job Title

Did you see her at Mathathawese Nightclub?
Don't for one moment think she wanted to drink

Recall she likes to talk about the dangers of drinking
Not only that-- she likes talking about things, people

The last time I checked, she wasn't a sexual predator, no!
Thus she wasn't doing some solicitation at that popular spot

The last time I checked, she wasn't given to spreading out her legs
She had a stomach-turning knack for spreading something though, yes!

I`m told her ex- best friend once said if she had a way she would make it
A point that Marvellous` passport page had *rumour-monger* for designation

Ungratefulness Stirs Up Bitter Truths

They said they didn`t expect him to suddenly
become a good old boy . He couldn't suddenly
become a saint after a prefect`s chair was suddenly
wrestled away from me. Thud! It must`ve been painful.

They said they didn't expect him to suddenly do holy things
as if he were working toward some momentous canonisation.
He was entitled to his rants, but they reminded him of his foothill
of crimes against humanity which even senility couldn't shake off.

Why She Was Afraid

I
2012.
It was not difficulty to see them----
those difficulties, deviations and disappointments.

II
A lone bystander, she was.
From a distance she saw romantic perturbations.

III
2011.
Before that. It was a different game ball.

IV
Alone she had taken strolls to gorgeous valleys and parks.
 There she would see what she thought epitomised
 unwavering attractiveness and togetherness.

V
She thought the beautiful arms of oneness and charm
were not on the surface.
She thought they had an undying life of their own inside lovebirds.

VI
She believed she heard a sound of their innermost engines,
that sound had its own undying heart.

VII
But then she saw romantic, seismic waves instead of warm hugs.
She heard them too. Taunting tornadoes.

VIII
She vowed she was not going to feel them.
Her grandma used to say each relationship or marriage had an ocean floor
which moved up and down ---just like when plates of the earth's crust heaped
on top of one another!
 She swore to herself that nothing else but bliss would nestle on her crust.
After all, was love not about committing oneself to caring and pleasing
forever?
She wondered where the scenic valleys with their promises and pride were.
She was of the opinion that the valleys and parks were calm and beautiful.

Permanently.

IX
A lone bystander, she was.
From a distance she saw a deadly deviation from beauty.
From normal to something else, from regular to an irregularity.
From hugs to hate, from heaven to hell. NO!
From a path of harmony to an alleyway of disharmony.
 She could see that that the participants were feeling
sudden violent shakings of the ground. It was scary.

X
Those were the diet and dances of mountains and countries
by virtue of the movements within the earth's crust--
some volcanic action, some earth tremor.

XI
But alas the heart has its own crust too---
at times it experiences its tsunamis and earthquakes
as a result of unsavoury and unfortunate movements
within its skin, its eyes and ears, its layer, its everything.

XII
2017.
When she fell victim to the sound of her heart--
she was unafraid and unashamed like a wildlife adventurer.
"My amount of faith will save our boat from capsizing or shaking violently.
Our boat will float on our ocean of love till we reach the shores of our
lives".
XIII
 She could not be aloof from love. No fear of an ache could
stand in her way. *Hey girl, helm it.* Love sailed her heart.
Her heart steered her body. Bliss danced in her soul.

XIV
It was as if she were going to be immune to the shifts and swings
of life. Together they skippered the boat.

 XVI
There was a stubborn air to it. A lifetime commitment. A faith.
As their boat sailed and sailed, wavy ups and downs nudged them.
As if saying: *everything real must be experienceable somewhere.*

At the Mercy of Legitimacy

massive lands were taken
by force from the indigenous peoples

then years later some lands were taken
by force by the landless and the powerful

when will this land drama come to a stop
because land is a people`s spirituality and dignity?

Farming Equipment and Commitment

Farms, fight for people`s prosperity,
refuse to be massaged or grabbed
by those who are rapists of land

Farms, many will come to you
and say we are farmers,
but beware of fools too

For fools farm poverty
till sleepiness
and barrenness
harvest excuses

Suspicious Agenda

Cracked floors fight against beauty and peace
Non-existent ablution facilities facilitate health disasters
Leaking roofs invite in droplets and climatic caprices
Burst sewage pipes tend to advance a smelly agenda

Humanity Is Sacred

Today…

there is a sea of challenges facing humanity
some people have gone for convenience
instead of magnificence

the sacredness of life
has been thrown out of the window
in the false preservation and pampering of self and us

humanity has lost the path to peace and dignity and equity
as beastly bigotry is given acres and acres
of leverage to break hearts

hearts are pounding as the temperatures run riot
and disdain is held back in an exercise in futility
things cannot be taken for granted anymore

A Call To Steer Towards Monetary Normalcy

Hope we are *fast* crawling
from under the table of terrible tangles and abuses
toward all the ideal lights and rights under the sky

In the past
bearer cheques and queues lurked in banking halls like cobras
while workers slept outside banks like begging vagrants

In the present
bond notes, cash corruption and cash shortages rule supreme--
feasibly-- the few, commissioned crawling trains envy high-speed ones in
Morocco!

Food For Thought

to swig because
something is given
is to tempt and test
the patience of such
comrades as Sir Vomit
or Constipation too far
like a silly bare tongue
kissing Ms. Electricity

to dance to the tune
of a sick fire is only musical
when the extinguishers
and firemen are working

to make a series of turnarounds
till one is really dizzy and does
not know where and how to stop
is to have an upside-down dream
whose closest relative is Nightmare

In The Pricky and Tricky Shoes of the Victims

His name was Trust
Though no one trusted him

A club of thugs was doing bloodcurdling acts
Usurping the innocent people`s cattle and land

Beating up hardworking owners and herders of the cattle
There was bloodshed and all the prints of mad destruction

One day vociferous and violent Trust fell out of favour with the club leaders
The thug was hounded and horrified as the club swooped on his cattle and
land

Walk A Mile In Their Shoes

they spat her out fast
like salty and smelly
and filthy phlegm

out she was flung
after saying things
like a lost missile

from hero to zero
from champ to crap
from fighter to fake

that's when I saw
that's when I agreed
that bigotry is bullshit

people can hug it
folks can hide it
but it's a cancer

that turns `round
not only to haunt but
also to eat up the keeper

I never thought
in this day and age
there was such a man

it turned out he was a moron
living on his moon of mischief
saying ladies from the other side

are mere sex-dolls and tools
to achieve his domination goals
and a sinister dilution agenda

that was in line with a bigger agenda
of denigration and swallowing up
and distortion of history and reality

souls lashed out at his impetuous antics
and insults and told him to pace a mile
in the shoes of the victims and women

than to seek to resuscitate a fallacy
or revive a long-known lie from death
because his calls were unconsciousness

I`ve never seen such courage and outrage
when they said he was an unused sperm
I knew he had brewed a sleeping storm

Wheels Are Still Off

In Lupane they saw the storm
as it swept through several villages--
viciously leaving behind a trajectory
of fatalities and miseries in its wake.

Up to this very day the powerful culprits –
for their part in those tragedies and sins ---
seek to blow away the haunting footprints
of melancholies, by all means possible.

Threats have proved to be detrimental
as they have a tendency to filter away
to the press or to the wrong people
or to catch up with one later in life.

 It has proved to be a clear exercise in futility
because of the clear absence of the wheels
of honesty, transparency and justice--
as these are essential ingredients.

In the first place, who was responsible
for stirring up and steering that storm –
which the helpless or- hapless villagers—
learnt later--was a cleaning tempest?

They heard that the storm
was no ordinary one, as it was also
referred to as an insecticide or DDT
by none other than its administrators!

Contrary to the fact that these chemicals
are to be used against niggling cockroaches,
innocent villagers saw their kin and kith
perish like flies receiving an insecticide spray.

It dawned on them that the DDT powder
was not going to deal with all species of roach
that stir up troubles in their various homes—
but was an atrocity set alight on the villagers!
That DDT powder, that cleaning storm

was unleashed on young and old villagers,
on babies born and unborn, on girls and women--
pregnant or not, the innocent souls were not spared.

Over the years since the horrors of that storm-- the business
of ducking and dodging over the DDT issue has been rampant---
with the administrators throwing melodramatic live snakes
at each other as they seek to hide behind a lone finger.

That storm, which was not only a pesticide
but, by all definitions also a genocide
has seen some culprits seeking to entomb
their heinous past activities and decisions.

Like drivers who were entrusted and tasked
with the role of safeguarding the precious lives
of the passengers, they crushed villagers to death---
forgetting that in the future they would need them.

Now, owing to the dynamics of life and power,
they hunger for votes from the same people
whose relatives` lives they stole away into
shallow graves, as they preach reconciliation!

They condemn the past, and admit it was a time
ruled by decay, damage and international isolation---
but they are not honest enough to disclose and accept
the extent to which they contributed to all that fracas.

They preach a gospel of forwardness while
 posing, smiling, smoking the peace pipe--
but the wheels of justice which came off long
ago are in the shallow graves and will not grovel
at their posturing, or speeches or kowtow to them!

Forget We Ever Met

Thulani knew that as a poor clerk from a village
in Gwanda, his intention to impress his new lover
in the capital city wasn't going to a bite of a delicacy.

For him to get a job in that city was a mammoth task,
in fact, he had to beg and grease someone`s itchy palms
with some borrowed funds to land that office contract.

As if their love spoke a language called Cashnglish
Thulani `s partner doubted his ability to spoil her,
already her eyes focused on his "charge of parsimony".

 Thulani`s extended family members in Gwanda expected
him to visit them with some Christmas goodies and clothes,
they didn't know his new sweetheart had other ideas and plans.

When he visited her a day before his intended departure for Gwanda
he had two presents for her: a gold wrist watch and a shiny mobile phone—
"What!! This is meretricious ornamentation, I want something of substance."

The rebuff was too hostile a dose for Thulani, but he tried to steady himself,
"I'm sorry, my beautiful bae, I had to thank and repay my HR manager,"
But those words didn't pacify her, so Thulani shot back," I give up!"

It Shouldn't Be Here

As one walks along that highway, its name becomes a reminder
of a long history of massacres, madness , dishonour and decay.

Robert Mugabe Way. What an insult. What an anomaly in Bulawayo.
It cannot be a part of the ethos of the residents who deserve peace.

Bulawayo says no to Genocide. *Robert Mugabe Way*. It`s time to find
your way to a distant domicile. In Zvimba you won`t be an imposition.

Maybe, a symbol of development and heroism. In Bulawayo, you`re
a villainous name. And unwelcome cemetery of justice and healing.

To the residents whose relatives were mass-murdered, you`re nothing
else but the *Robbing Way* . All they clamour for is the *Freedom Way*.

If Africa Has To Prosper

They do more than just accepting bribes,
you will remember one former first lady
who it is allegedly siphoned ivory tusks
under the pretext of giving away gifts?

That is just 1 kilogram of sugar in a bag
of 100 000 000 kilograms of the same stuff--,
the report on the plunderers---or what one
may call the modern merciless colonialists

makes for a raw read for more than one reason.
These elite African oligarchs are not only bent on
hindering the development of governance systems---
they always safeguard their loot by externalizing it.

By extracting their wealth from their countries
and keeping it beyond the borders of the continent,
there is a thin line between the former colonialists`
agendas and those of some of today's black leaders.

No wonder some of them are despicable liabilities at home,
but dependable health tourists out there- since their sons
and daughters are crowned beneficiaries of overseas education,
medical treatment, luxurious foreign trips ,holidays and residences.

Of Old Hegemonic Habits

Last time Thebe checked the news
the national broadcasting station
had not changed much in terms
of content and programming

Save for the two faces
which viewers had come
to accept as nothing but
facetious faces of propaganda

Those two had become somehow
invisible and less and less
relevant except when they
appeared as foul faces

Coverage of news
was by and large
still biased –a one
party campaign kit

Persecuted For Justice

Did you hear of the peaceful activists who were stalked
and captured and arrested fast?
Did you?
When will we have a true dawn of democracy and justice?
Reconciliation?
I ask you
How is it born under such skewed and unjust conditions?
Maybe abortion
Why is it a crime to exercise one`s constitutional right
to demonstrate against infamous butchers of innocent souls?
Why?
Is it because the infamous slayers trivialise the lives of others?
Of the butchered victims' relatives too?
Not to mention the authorities' glaring disrespect for justice!
Is it because the powerful slaughters seek to sweep
them under the rug?
I mean are they are so mighty and mean that they want to bury
their evil atrocities too?
How?
Did you hear their sanctimonious calls?
Do the dead forget and forgive?
How?
In their shallow graves?
Atrocities
Who is honestly taking responsibility for them in the first place?
The arrests
Did you see the highhandedness and swiftness of the authorities?
Did you?
If the economic woes were being dealt with that rapidity--
would we still be stuck with liquidity problems as a country?
I ask
Is cash readily available now?
Tell me
Why can`t the authorities arrest the economic challenges—
not the innocent activists?
Atrocities
As long as they are not properly addressed ,do you think
these will stop peeping and weeping from under the carpet?

Tell me
Atrocities
Atrocities
Atrocities are not the poor victims` stupidities
So can they be wished away just like that?

Proliferation In The Wrong Place

wearing lugubrious expressions
tattered trousers and shorts
toe-popping out socks and shoes

unemployed masses marched
to the authorities demanding
one thing and one thing only

-- space for industrial activity--
they claimed they liked churches
but factories couldn't be cathedrals

they had seen an economic incongruity
during the reign of the unseated strongman
where the industrial site was idle or "churchified"

placard-carrying protesters presented their petition
the bunch had young and old graduates and traders
jobs! not jokes and economic yokes!--they vocalised

Moving Onto Higher Ground

tell me tell me
what will lift us
out of the deep ocean currents
and carry us gently and gently
through the waves of stupidity
and arrogance and ignorance
till we reach the land of love
with a weather so favourable
so that we could get a feel of
and see the ship of our dreams
come with savings and calm?

From Subjugation To Emancipation

She had paddled through muddy waters
Of crude enchainment and enslavement

Nonkululeko had lived a dejected life
Of acidic incarceration and submission

In her 42 years she had known no liberty
She was fluent in the language of captivity

She was a foreigner to her family`s norms
An introverted beggar to her father`s wealth

Her world was far from self and self-sufficiency
It was about her husband and them and them only

Her eldest brother arrived and preached the gospel
Of release and self-confidence and self-determination

He told her that he was taking her back to their home
For Nonkululeko home seemed to be a big pipedream

How could she leave behind her children and her abuser?
Her brother told her to leave everything and her unfreedom

And so they set out on the long hard journey to KoMthwa
And slowly but surely a big pipedream became her freedom

A Different Tune

the good admirers were at it again
vowing to show solidarity
and unity

being associated with awful cruelty
they promised to march
in support of their idol

years later when the man was history
the same admirers didn't memorialize
the accomplishments of their hero

like chameleons they adapted
to the tongue of his successor
and hailed his belated arrival

they sang different songs
which rapped the forerunner
as a cruel mischief-maker

As If They Didn't Know

was our unkind king frog
nocturnal in nature?
they asked when
he had been ferried away

he spent most of the day
snoozing in his citadel
hidden amongst gold
and lies and loot

was our unkind king frog
gregarious in nature?
they asked when
he was unable to croak

he travelled with countless frogs
to many foreign ponds and lakes
he liked lounging in the exotic
meadows and wetlands too

did our unkind king frog
have a sensual soprano voice?
they asked
as if they didn't know

he was active in the evenings
and at night :inflating his throat
pouch about the urgent need
to protect our lakes and ponds

did our unkind king frog
protect our lakes and ponds?
they asked
as if they didn't know

Wondering about Nocturnal Wanderings

they say he was pollinated by mad moths
polluted by pride and pretensions
he lived a life of bats and owls
his flowers followed a pattern
of opening during the night
and closing at daylight

From City To Rusticity

They sought to escape
the distractions of a busy life,
the bustles and hustles of the city;
Then they packed their bags, off they
went with their wondering cats and dogs
 to the remotest of villages where they hoped
to become farmers of simplicity and tranquillity

Haunted By His Mentor`s Disastrous Ghost

What people needed was an exhibition of maturity
in the analysis of events unfolding so said one voice--
Was it not too early to say they had safely arrived
in the land of plenty and promise?
Had their prayers not been answered?

Did people not clamour for a saviour
who would usher in a new era
of hope and progress and love
and close an unholy chapter
of miseries and madness?

They said there was a saviour
and liberator on the scene
 because cash was oozing
out of ATMs like in the old
days before collapse ruled.

But many said apply brakes citizens--
This is not our complaint but restraint!
Did the saviour bring up wise ideas before?
Can he captain our altruistic ship to prosperity
when he was part and parcel of the rot that sank it?

Some said the liberator was a disciple of the oppressor--
Wait a minute? What? The real product of a rotten system!
Were they not in that mess because of his master`s inanities?
How could they exonerate him because he nurtured and midwifed
Those unprecedented offences and decadences over princely decades?

Others said optimism was their hymn because any change was something--
Didn't people want CHANGE? Why were people ungrateful and negative?
Couldn't they accept the bold declarations he had made as a new broom?
Many said if he had possibly reformed and learnt from their transgressions--
then those were confessions they didn't want to hear but see in practice!

Agent Of One`s Socialisation

I refuse, I do with conviction---
The fallacy that writers are agents
Of foreign powers and principalities

I stoutly reject, I do with the force
Of an injured LION in the woodlands
The dead politics of appeasement

Who are the guardians and chroniclers
Of their society's history and heritage?
Are they not the scribes and historians?

They say the West dictates what writers
Should say or write—maybe in competitions?
I haven't heard them tell me to write about wars

I know proper writers to be agents of positive change
To be surgeons of their communities and consciences
To be thermometers and stethoscopes of their societies

Why should anyone from far remind me that I am hungry?
Why should anyone from far tell me that there is subjugation?
Am I not human enough to feel hunger or repel against an injustice?

I see officials shouting hoarse about the presence of shadows
I don't see a willingness to confront issues of justice and unity
They decide to see distant shadows at the expense of their bigotry

The Bambazonke Syndrome

The little history I know about Aunt NakaThembelihle
is that she was a school teacher and an activist of sorts.
She taught both in the urban and rural areas of the country.
During her active years in education and after retirement
she advocated for the protection and promotion of the youth,
chiefly those infected by AIDS ,or with albinism ;or the abused.
She used to watch nearly 100% of Highlanders matches in Zim.

Aunt NakaThembelihle visited us a few days ago, what a lively chat
we had over a number of issues. Dynamic as ever, she told me how
she used to support her favourite soccer club through its lows or highs.
What strike me is the fact that she is an old lady who follows what is
happening around the country in particular and the world in general.
A nonagenarian, she still exhibits a measure of smartness in terms
of observational skills in spite of her poor sight and diabetic state.

Of all the three daughters of my aunty, none is a nurse but she
is disheartened by the government`s recent decision to sack
15 000 nurses for engaging in a strike action. "I`ve always stood
with those in dire straits, in destitution, in distress , those
whose plight and grievances are ignored or brushed aside.
I supported the liberation war fighters for the same reason.
Today, I stand in solidarity with the dismissed nurses. *Nx* !"

A frequent visitor to the myriad of the country`s public health
bodies, she believes paralysis has turned them into death traps.
"In the past, do you know that Luveve Clinic had specialists and
all the equipment and drugs you could think of? Now, it's sad,
big hospitals like Mpilo are devoid of basic drugs! You then expect
nurses are who are owed monies, are underpaid, underequipped
to work as if everything`s fine. That`s clowning. Where`s sanity?"

She said everybody has a right to life and a fair trial, not what
she called the Bambazonke Games which we are being exposed
to on a daily basis. "What do you mean, auntie?" I enquired.
"I`ve never been a big fan of the Bambazonke mentality. It`s delusional.
It`s a self-serving mentality which falsely assumes that one has a right
to grab everything, anywhere, anyhow. A win-win affair for oneself
without compromises. It breeds a false sense of entitlement and pride."

We discussed sports again, only this time she was telling me how proud over the years she has been of the performances and pedigree of the national cricket team. "Your cousin, Thembelihle who has lived in India and other countries says when foreigners introduce cricket as a subject for discussion she looks them in the eye, and takes them head-on. Why? It`s one of the few sports in which we`ve made a name for ourselves. On that note, I stand with Health Streak. I smell a scapegoating hand of the Bambazonke syndrome .Hope cricket won`t be the loser".

Wringing and Scheming Hearts

it was a rather frosty Wednesday morning
ten-ish ,her moves had a sluggish touch to them

vacuuming, humming, tidying up the living room
the least thing she expected was a serpent

 there it was
long, lazy, gliding on the floor, at the wall`s edge

"sekaNe, a snake, under the sofa!" she yelled
 he leapt up

and made several nervous attempts at slicing up
the risky reptile but it kept on slithering away

when the intruder was finally chopped apart
with a block from a disused wooden room divider

and ferried lifeless in a yellow plastic bag and dumped
in a grassy and bushy area of the suburb, echoes started

they bare happiness and smiles when you buy those things
but I know deep inside them their hearts are bleeding spite

how does a snake enter a closed room and hide under a sofa
on a tiled and cold floor, and when did it enter?—"aunt" doubted

one theorist guessed the intruder could have entered the room
earlier during the day or during the evening when the door was open

that neighbour who called herself a real realist and the wife`s real aunt
(by the way, everyone is everybody `relative in the high-density suburbs!)

was not convinced by the theorist `s assumptions surrounding the snake saga
how does a snake enter a room without anybody seeing it, is this a snake
really?

the theorist said he was not an expert in the affairs and behaviours of snakes
but he knew that a snake could sense and follow the presence of rodents

the man of the house expressed his doubts saying he was shocked
the next day to discover that the bag was no longer at the dumpsite!

that was not a mere snake, forget about open or closed doors,
the owner of that snaky trinket must have fetched it, "aunt" said

Finally

It was not just a monumental mountain
It was an institution and a big fountain

When it comes to issues of development
We are talking of a monumental disaster

When it comes to policies and legacies, what a pity
It was an institution whose stamp is a cesspit

If ever there was a fountain of oppression
It was its untouchable sanctuary and idol

It was more of an error than an era
It was more of an abortion than an admin

Its hellish heroism bordered on hedonism
It had no placenta or place in Pan-Africanism

Its invincibility has fallen but not its insidiousness
For it was an institution of pollution and abomination

Placards

Placards! Placards! Placards!
Go ye to monster-land, leave my motherland!
Sellouts and tea-oldies, time up!
Fossils are too fat to fit in with time.
Companies have closed down, please close shop!
Castrate rapists, criminalize fat-cat activities.
Save us from Savage Garbage of any age.

Deep In Thought

A job was chested down to Shokoa
Even if he had an odour of lapses
There was a series of mental hiatuses
He thought of himself as a think tank
Or possibly he didn't feel his stink
At work he was having a nightmare
What kind of a manager sleeps on the job!
At home his stamina couldn't cope
With the demands of his five wives
At night he couldn't sleep soundly
Because he was drunk with thought
 He tried every trick in the Unholy
Book of Hoaxes and Foxes to no avail

Once a fire he was a drained little wire
Ultimately he resembled a tiny zombie
And felt the biggest of quarantines ever

The Long List

a college principal was handed a long list
with names to 'process' for the year`s intake

the order was clear and loud: process the list
last year the instruction was: sort out the list

he knew that in spite of the difference in wording
the message was the same: enrol all these students

the order was from nameless but shameless sources
troubled about ethics and fairness he studied the list

it was a fact that even when it came to jobs or other
opportunities the invisible and sinister forces lingered

it was always the case there that the self-crowned victors
always rammed things down the throats of their hapless victims

it did not give him a peace of mind that a beast always reared its ugly
head depicting the owners of things on one side and the beggars on the other

he hated with a passion the idea of being taken as a perpetual minnow and
beggar
he wondered how he could wipe out the thickening line between somebodies
and nobodies

why should there be some much suppression and polarisation and tension?
what about long lists of atrocities and lies and bootlicking and grandstanding?

was he going to condemn the local students to hell again
because suddenly there was another divisive, imposed list?

that day his conscience and integrity told him: say no or resign
he dragged himself home and spent a prayerful and wakeful night

the following day when the head of the compiler of the list phoned him
he took him by surprise by declaring: I`m a professional I won`t process it!

the compiler pondered and paused and when the principal tried to ask him
whether he had a problem with his stance there was no word from the bigot

the following morning the papers were awash with the corrupt official's story-
-
one headline screamed: BIGOTRY SUCCUMBS TO A STROKE OF
BRAVERY

A Loud Silence

there a loud silence wafting through
where nothing is quite as it seems
only the tallest trees feel the wind

there is sweet bitterness being tasted
where nothing is quite as it seems
only the gratified feast on melodies

there is milk and honey
where nothing is quite as it seems
only the chosen are the drinkers and eaters

 there is harmony and happiness
where nothing is quite as it seems
only for the blind beneficiaries and lickers

there is choice and progress
where nothing is quite as it seems
only fear and favouritism are the game plans

a village living by its own rules and norms
parents at the beck and call of children
cats roaring under chicken fowls

victims toiling in vain and in silence
orphans living in abject poverty
whispers packaged in fear

there is intellectual insolvency
where nothing is quite as it seems
only the greasing of palms rules supreme

there is a wealth of truth
where nothing is quite as it seems
its skyscrapers of lies stink up to the heavens

 there is pleasing calmness
where nothing is quite as it seems
only a can of worms cannot be deceived

there is a hyped lustre
where nothing is quite as it seems
its rustiness and nastiness gleams in potholes

there is spotlessness
where nothing is quite as it seems
its dirtiness rots under luminous rugs

there is something
where nothing is quite as it seems
it is a loud silence wafting through…

Glossary

AU: African Union

Bhalagwe Camp: was the most notorious detention centre of all which was situated just west of the Antelope Mine. During the Gukurawundi atrocities, victims were subjected brutal interrogation, torture and killings by the North Korean-trained soldiers of the ZANU PF government.

Ndebele: The Northern Ndebele people are a Bantu nation and ethnic group in Southern Africa, who share a common Ndebele culture and Ndebele language.

MDC: Movement For Democratic Change, one of Zimbabwe`s political parties.

The Gukurahundi was a series of massacres of Ndebele civilians.

A gukurahundist is a person who planned or participated in such massacres or someone who harbours or supports such ideas ,acts, policies and practices of supremacy

Gukurahundism is a system of governance which thrives on supremacist policies and practices. It encompasses attitudes, programmes and procedures aimed at denying Non-Shona citizens access to equitable employment, educational, cultural, linguistic and business opportunities as if they do not deserve full citizenship rights

Mthwakazi is the traditional name of the proto-Ndebele and Ndebele kingdom

PDP: People's Democratic Party, one of Zimbabwe`s political parties

Zim is short for Zimbabwe

SADC: Southern African Development Community

Shona: a group of peoples inhabiting parts of southern Africa. The Shona comprise over three quarters of the population of Zimbabwe.

ZANU PF:Zimbabwe`s African Union- Patriotic Front

ZAPU:Zimbabwe African People`s Union

ZIPRA:Zimbabwe People`s Revolutionary Army. It was ZAPU`s army.

Printed in the United States
By Bookmasters